Rock 'n' Roll
&
Comic Books
Taught Me
All I Know

Essays by

Rob Errera

Editorial guidance by Nancy Rubenstein, Christa Limone, and Ken
Kimmel.

Cover design and interior art by Dominic Wilde.

For Michael. Brother. Friend.

Table of Contents

THE DUMBEST THING(S) I'VE EVER DONE

January 2019

The story I'm about to relate has pained me for well over three decades, and it will pain you too, even if you're not a musician or a comic book fan. It's a story about being young and stupid.

When I was sixteen, I sold all of my worldly possessions to get a custom guitar built for me. Doesn't sound like a big deal—many young kids save up their summer job money for a big purchase, like a car, or a guitar, or college text books. But I didn't have typical teenage worldly possessions. My stuff was *good*, world class collectors' items. I just didn't know and/or appreciate their true value.

I became a comic book collector in 1980, at the tender age of twelve. Before that I was merely a comic book reader. Once I finished an issue, I'd toss it into a big, cardboard box. My brother and I sorted through the box whenever we needed reading material. Mike liked *The Mighty Thor,* while I preferred *The Incredible Hulk* and anything with monsters. Always monsters. We both thought *Prince Namor, the Sub-Mariner,* was a sissy. Between 1974 and 1980, our box-o-comics got pretty full.

I met a kid in middle school who liked comic books, too. Rich invited me over to his house to look at his collection. His comics were in a box, too, but each issue was carefully bagged in plastic with a protective cardboard backing board. What was this? He also showed me a copy of Robert Overstreet's Comic Book Price Guide.

"I have some old issues of *Detective Comics* from my uncle that are worth fifty bucks each!" he boasted. I was impressed. Could my old box of comics be valuable? (Brother Mike had moved on to college, leaving me sole proprietorship over the musty comic book box.)

I got my own copy of Overstreet's Price Guide. Most of our old comic books were pretty beat up from being read and re-read so often, but issues #180-181 of *The Incredible Hulk* were collector's items because they introduced a new character named Wolverine. I wasn't impressed with Wolverine—he certainly wasn't as menacing as the fanged, clawed, hairy Wendigo, whom Hulk was battling before Wolverine showed up. But I followed Wolverine over to the newly re-vamped *X-Men.*

Rich and I got after-school and summer jobs picking and planting strawberries at a local farm and delivering newspapers. Each week we'd invest the bulk of our meager paychecks into comic books.

For a young douchebag, I had impeccable taste. Rich and I would scour local comic book shops and weekend shows for rare back issues. I picked up issues of *Swamp Thing* and old E.C. Comics, like *Haunt Of Fear* and *Tales From The Crypt.* Both Rich and I enjoyed the work of writer/artist Frank

Miller, and we collected every issue of *Daredevil* and *Batman* he worked on. I bought a page of original Frank Miller art from *Daredevil #160*.

In a few short years, I had amassed a nice comic book collection. The crown jewel was *X-Men Giant Size #1*, which my parents bought me for Christmas 1980 for $60. It was the most valuable comic book I owned.

But something drew me away from the bang-smash-crash world of superheroes and supervillains. It was the howl of feedback and the scent of perfume—rock 'n' roll…and girls.

***

The owner of the local music store was named Morris and his wife was Debbie. They had a baby that crawled—and later toddled—around the music store while teens with rock-star dreams filed in-and-out for guitar lessons and to play the new merchandise.

Morris' Music Store had a quaint, homey feel. My friends and I bought all our gear there. It was a haul to Sam Ash— especially when you needed Mom to drive you. We could ride our bikes to Morris'. Thinking back on it, the patronage of my friends and I probably kept Morris in business. Morris closed up shop soon after we all got our drivers licenses, and started traveling to the big New York City music stores.

I once ordered a Dean Markley 60-watt tube amplifier from Morris. The wrong model was delivered, and I wanted Morris to return it for one with built-in reverb. Morris looked ready to cry.

"Look, I already paid for this amplifier, and I don't have the credit to return it," he said, looking sad and disgusted that he had to explain his financial troubles to a 16-year-old suburban kid who didn't understand and didn't care. I just wanted dreamy reverb in my over-priced amplifier.

But Morris convinced me to buy the non-reverb model. Morris convinced me to do a lot of things. My friends and I trusted him. He was a cool "older guy" (maybe thirty?) that supported the arts! His wife played guitar!

I bought my first "real" guitar at Morris' Music—a used Gibson SG, circa 1967. It wasn't original. The pickups were changed (to DiMarzios, I think), the tuners were swapped out (to Grovers), and someone had painted the guitar cherry red. The instrument cost $225.

Today such a classic instrument, even one repainted, with non-original parts, could easily fetch five to ten times that price. But in the early 1980s it was not uncommon to find used Gibsons and Fenders in the $300-$500 range. Such instruments were a great investment…if you were smart enough to keep them.

I got a mirrored pickguard for my SG because Glenn Tipton from Judas Priest played an SG with a mirrored pickguard. Then I switched the pickguard to black, which looked better against the red. It was an awesome guitar, but it was 15 years old (a year older than me at the time) and it needed new frets. The old frets were worn and nicked, and I broke strings frequently.

Not only did I learn to play "Sweet Home Alabama" and "Smoke On The Water" on that old Gibson, that instrument led me to a land from which I've never returned. Guitars are a drug. They soothe. They comfort. They make you feel good. They make you want more. Guitars are addictive, and that old Gibson SG was my first high.

No "serious player" has just one guitar. You need to have an acoustic *and* an electric guitar, at the very least. Once you get an electric guitar, you'll want one with single coil pickups (like a Fender) and another with humbucking pickups (like a Gibson). In the early '80s, everybody needed a heavy metal machine with a locking tremolo system that could imitate the sound of crashing airplanes and inhuman screams.

Soon you'll branch out to a jazzy hollow-body, or something crazy like an Explorer or Flying V. Every guitar sounds, plays, and feels unique. Five Fender Stratocasters will all play and sound differently. Guitars are like souls, each distinct and beautiful, offering an individual voice to the world.

Guitars are like women, too—from the feel of their bodies pressed against yours, to the caress of their long, smooth necks, to the sound hole—feminine and sensual. And variety is the spice of life.

The quest to find *your* guitar, that one perfect instrument that is your musical soulmate, lies at the heart of my teenage stupidity. I thought I could build the perfect musical mate, but you can't. Your guitar won't change over time, but *you* will.

Money and finances are not my strong suit, and in my early teens I was completely clueless about the value of a dollar. I wanted money, so I got a job. I had no expenses, so everything I earned was funneled into comic books. I spent thousands on comic books during the early 1980s.

I wasn't fiscally responsible. I spent everything I made; didn't bank a penny. Paychecks only needed to last a week until the next one came along. I lived paycheck-to-paycheck long before I lived on my own, long before I had a family to care for, but it's a bad/dangerous/irresponsible habit that endures to this day. I'm still a lousy saver.

My adolescent mind considered my comic purchases investments. Sure, I bought a lot of crappy comic books, but many of the titles I collected—*Batman, Daredevil, X-Men*, and *The New Teen Titans*—were experiencing a golden age of storytelling and artwork. My collection would have been

9

worth a pretty penny.

If I had kept it.

Music (and girls…always monsters…always girls) changed everything. Brother Mike had an acoustic guitar and an awesome record collection, everything from Zappa to Zeppelin, Fleetwood Mac, David Bowie, Grateful Dead…each was a roadmap to cool, an audio soundscape that shaped my tender ears and young mind. I'll always be indebted to my brother for introducing me to these cornerstones of rock music (and, sometimes, the strange fringes of the genre).

As I came of age during the 1980s, this musical foundation revealed a sad, basic truth: Music was getting worse. The new bands of the 1980s simply weren't as *good* as the groups from a decade earlier. Synthesizers and fake drums ushered in a barren wasteland of soulless songs. There were few exceptions. The post-New Wave, jangly alternative sound of U2, REM, and The Cure was catchy, but lacked the oomph of '70s power rock.

The only bastion left for "oomph rock" was heavy metal, and I put all of my denim-and-leather clad eggs in the hard rock basket. Metallica, Ozzy, Iron Maiden, Van Halen, and Judas Priest paved the way for a legion of Spandex-wearing hair bands which tried to capture the sound of 1980s teen angst and testosterone. Yeah, it was screamy and cheesy, but at least the guitar players strived for a high level of technical achievement and musicianship. At least these bands wrote their own songs and played real instruments.

Change happens fast when you're a teenager. One moment you're baby-smooth, the next you've got a hairy crotch and armpits. My friendship with Rich—and the love of comic books we shared—began to fade. By sophomore year of high school I had a new group of friends, all of whom were musicians. We formed bands, broke-up, and reformed.

Music became the driving force in our lives, and Morris' Music Shop was our local house of worship.

***

When I was 15 years old, my grandmother died. My mother gave me $500.

"This is from your Grandmother," she said. "She would want you to do something smart with it, like put it in the bank for college. But it's *your* money to do with as you'd like."

I knew exactly what to do with it. There was a used '68 Gibson Les Paul hanging in Morris' Music Shop, faded cherry sunburst, just like Jimmy Page's guitar. The owner wanted exactly $500 for it.

"Everything's original," Morris said as I strummed the guitar through the store amp. "Those pickups alone are worth $500!"

That convinced me. Morris was so *convincing!* I handed over my cash and walked out of Morris's with the Les Paul. Thank you, Grandma Nellie! By the end of 1983, I owned an all-original '68 Les Paul, a '67 modified SG, and several long boxes of collectible comic books. (Sadly, relegated to the back of my closet. Comics were kid stuff. Heavy metal was for grown-ups!)

If I could time travel, I'd visit myself in 1983, toss my old Gibsons in the closet next to the comic books, and nail the door shut. Then I'd beat myself with the hammer.

Because as smart as my purchases were when it came to guitars and comic books, my next choices were very, *very* stupid.

Shortly after my sixteenth birthday, my friend Mark and I decided Morris should build us custom guitars. We were

11

both enamored with a Lake Placid blue Stratocaster Morris built for his wife. Morris could build us guitars so cool, we'd *never* need to buy another guitar *ever* again!

We priced the projects out. Bodies and necks would cost us a few hundred, electronics and metal-friendly Kahler locking tremolos a few hundred more. Toss in the cost of assembly and a custom Morris paint job, and our guitars each totaled around $1,200.

How could I afford such an expense? Save up a couple months' salary from my after school job at Burger King? Hell no! I needed immediate gratification.

I decided to strip the original Gibson PAF pickups out of my Les Paul. Hey, Morris said the pick-ups alone were worth $500! I replaced them with a pair of used DiMarzios (bought at Morris', of course). I'd put Les Paul pickups in my new, custom Super Strat and sell my SG and Les Paul to buy the guitar body and neck.

After lengthy deliberation I made a radical design choice. Instead of getting fancy, I'd have Morris paint the guitar a brilliant arctic white. This way my guitar's color would change along with the stage lights when I played Madison Square Garden.

Yuck. Boo.

In my hormone-addled teenage brain, it all made perfect sense. Everything was coming together.

***

In the pre-app days of the 1980s, items were bought and sold through the classified section of newspapers. One particular publication, *The Want Ad Press*, came out weekly and featured items for sale. I placed an ad offering my Les Paul and my SG, together, for $500.

Five hundred. For both.

Fail.

I figured the pick-ups I'd removed from the Les Paul were probably worth $225, and if I could sell the instruments for what I paid for them, I'd be up a free pair of classic pick-ups. Brilliant!

Even by 1983 prices, $500 was a steal for two old Gibsons. I was flooded with calls from interested buyers the day after my classified ad came out. The next day a long-haired metalhead showed up at my parents' house. I took the strange man downstairs to my bedroom. He strummed each guitar for about a minute and handed me $500.

"Great deal, dude!" he called over his shoulder as he strode down my parents' driveway, a guitar case in each hand. "Thanks!"

I took my $500 and my groovy Gibson PAF pickups down to Morris. This money would get me started, but I still needed several hundred more in order to finish the guitar.

***

I dug my comic book collection out of the closet and asked my Mom to drive me down to a musty used book shop in Passaic. I'd shopped there for years, and the sign over the front door claimed they bought comic books. "Bring us your whole collection!" the sign advised, but when I did—Mom helping me carry half-a-dozen long comic boxes into the store—the tired-looking man behind the counter was only interested in a handful of back issues.

"What's this?" he held up a page of original comic book art.

"An original Frank Miller page from *Daredevil*."

"Who?"

"Frank Miller. He's a writer…and an artist." A revolutionary comic book artist, as it turned out, who later brought his

13

unique vision to graphic novels and films like *300* and *Sin City*.

Comic Book Guy didn't know Frank Miller. He was slightly more impressed with my page of original Sal Buscema art from *Incredible Hulk*, but not much. He wasn't interested in my entire Hulk collection, just the issue with Wolverine. I insisted everything must go, from the crinkly old box-o-comics issues to the mint copies of *Batman* and *Daredevil.* Even *X-Men Giant Size #1*.

I insisted.

Comic Book Guy begrudgingly offered me $500 for the entire collection. We both knew he was ripping me off, but I took the money, eager to cash out my kiddie books to fully fund my rock 'n' roll fantasy.

***

I got what I wanted. I sold all of my worldly possessions to became the proud owner of a plain-but-pretty white Stratocaster-type guitar. Not an *actual* Fender Stratocaster, which would have held its value, but a Stratocaster-type copy. But it was all mine, custom-made, just for me. Me and my white Stratocaster would never part!

Within six months I was anxious to buy another guitar. The White Whale played and sounded nice...but not as nice as it should have. Morris messed up the installation of the bridge, and the high E-string tended to drift off the edge of the neck in the upper register. And the Gibson pickups, which sounded so wonderfully meaty inside the heavy mahogany Les Paul, lost much of their bite inside of the lighter Strat-style body. My wonderful instrument wasn't so wonderful after all, and it has cost me everything I owned to get it.

Where were my parents? I needed guidance, but shunned their involvement. They probably would have loaned me $500. Maybe even $1200. (Ok, probably not $1200.) But I wanted to do it on my own. I was a grown-up. I knew want I wanted, and I knew how to get it.

Now I build guitars with my teenage son. We make good guitars for $100, and world-class instruments for $500. So why did I pay Morris more than double that, thirty years ago, to build me a guitar that's not half as good?

Because I was a Grade-A asshole. Rock 'n' roll and comic books made me that way.

Rock 'n' roll and comic books taught me all I know.

Schooled By
Comic Books

THE INCREDIBLE HULK IS DEAD! LONG LIVE HULK!

July 2011

Growing up, *The Incredible Hulk* was my favorite comic book. But the big green galoot's run is coming to an end, and I'm not sorry to see him go.

The Incredible Hulk has a dark side that's haunted me since childhood.

Publisher Marvel Comics announced the 49-year-old title would end this August with issue #635. (Since nothing ever truly ends in the comic book universe, the green Goliath will still he-man his own title, simply called *Hulk*, which launched in 2008.)

The Hulk was the strongest of all superheroes. His brute strength was...well, incredible. But his power was tied to his temper. The Hulk's simple creed was, "The madder Hulk gets, the stronger Hulk gets!"

The comic book had a brilliant premise, creator Stan Lee's

combination of *Frankenstein* and *Dr. Jekyll and Mr. Hyde*.
Meek scientist Bruce Banner harbors a monster inside him, a
big green wrecking machine who comes out when Banner is
angry or stressed. Push pansy Bruce far enough, and he
transforms into a Not-So-Jolly Green Giant. Hulk smash!

Who among us wouldn't like to have that transformative
power on occasion? As a kid it represented a chance to right
a thousand injustices, a chance to tip the scales against
bullies, older kids, and adults.

But it was all a lie. Losing your temper never makes you
stronger. It makes you weaker. Lose your cool, and you lose
your advantage.

It took me a long time to learn this. I punched a lot of holes
in walls, and busted innumerable telephones over the years.
In 2003 I raged against an ATM machine, a stupid stunt that
cost me hundreds of dollars in fines and almost landed me in
jail. (Did you know there are *cameras* in those things?)

My temper has never worked to my advantage. Rob smash!
The only thing it ever got me was heartache, a reputation as
an overly emotional hothead, and multiple hand injuries.

I've finally managed to control my temper (well...I've
improved). I've mellowed with age, therapy, and medication.
It wasn't until recently that I began to wonder how much
growing up with *The Incredible Hulk* played into my violent
outbursts. I can't lay all the blame on the Jade Giant, but I
don't think following his temper-fueled adventures did me
much good as a kid. Unlike many superheroes, Hulk wasn't a
good role model.

Stan Lee created many memorable superheroes, characters
that were very human despite their special abilities. Daredevil
was blind. Spiderman was a high school geek. The X-Men
were all misfits—mutants—looking for a way to fit into
society. These Marvel heroes taught young readers respect,

hard work, and other basic building blocks of self-confidence.

But Hulk wasn't Hulk unless he lost his temper.

Some superheroes use their powers to enhance the lives of their alter egos. Peter Parker and Clark Kent always had great scoops for the newspapers they worked for. Daredevil would capture bad guys, and his alter ego, criminal attorney Matt Murdock, made sure they stayed in jail.

But Bruce Banner's superpower actually ruined his career as a brilliant scientist. Most storylines involved a few pages of Hulk smashing things up then leaving poor Bruce Banner to either pick up the pieces or run from authorities. Banner lived the life of a loner, a fugitive, no friends, no family, always on the run.

That's what a bad temper will get you.

I still love you, Hulk, but you need to chill out, man! Try a glass of wine and a scented candle. But even the incredible Hulk isn't strong enough to prop up Marvel's slumping comic books sales.

Rob Errera

POPULAR MARVEL UNIVERSE HAS AN UNCERTAIN CENTER

May 2017

As a boy, I was a Marvel comics man.

I bought three or four Marvel titles a month between the ages of 10 and 14, usually *Hulk, Thor*, and *X-Men*. In the early '80s there were essentially three choices at the comic book rack: Marvel superheroes, DC superheroes (*Batman, Superman, Wonder Woman*, etc.) or "kiddie comics" (*Archie, Richie Rich, Casper*, etc.).

Marvel Comics had the most vibrant characters and storylines at the time—so much so that Marvel's publishing heyday in the '80s still fuels the cinematic juggernaut known as the Marvel Universe today. There are 15 summer blockbusters set in the Marvel comic book universe, starting with 2008's *Iron Man* and running through *Guardians Of The Galaxy 2*, which opened to outstanding box office totals earlier this month. Another half-dozen Marvel movies are in production, and Hollywood shows no sign of slowing down

22

the superhero movie machine. (While the *X-Men* are Marvel characters, they're licensed to a different movie studio, so that franchise is not technically part of the Marvel movie universe.)

You'd think the box office success of Marvel movies would boost sales of Marvel comic books, but that's not the case. Marvel's biggest superhero comics—*Spiderman, Iron Man, Captain America*—all sell less than 50,000 copies a month. By comparison, DC's top superhero titles sell twice as many copies. Despite the success of the Marvel Universe on the big screen, the company's comic book line—the source material for its films—is in trouble.

Why?

Some blame poor business management and others blame weak editorial leadership. Some claim the company hasn't been right since Disney bought it in 2009. Even Marvel's own management seems confused about which direction to take. Marvel VP of sales David Gabriel made statements on Twitter recently suggesting the company's problems stem from its recent push into "diverse superheroes" (i.e., females and characters of color).

"That stuff doesn't sell," Gabriel said. "The market doesn't want these characters."

The following day, Forbes Magazine ran an article on Marvel's Editor-in-Chief Axel Alonso who emphasized the success of the company's new line of diverse charters. So which is it? And, more importantly, why are audiences flocking to theaters to see Marvel superhero movies, yet ignoring the comic books that inspire those films?

As a disciple of Marvel's '80s heyday, it's sad seeing such influential comic book source material flounder. (Good riddance to *Richie Rich*, however!) Such is the nature of comic book heroes—so many fade away with changes in the publishing industry. (I miss you most of all, Crypt Keeper.) At least the cinematic success of the Marvel Universe gives these classic characters new life beyond the four-color panels of printed comic books.

What comic book tops today's bestseller lists? The same title that tops the television ratings—*The Walking Dead*, published by Image Comics. Image was formed in 1992 by former Marvel and DC staffers who were tired of giving up the copyrights to the characters they created. Heed the harsh example of Stan Lee! 'Nuff said!

Poor Stan Lee. Marvel ripped him off. Most of the blockbuster superhero movies are based on characters and stories created by Stan back in the 1970s. Stan got a stipend (and allegations of elder abuse) while Marvel reaped the benefits of an empire. Now Stan's gone to that Big Marvelverse in the sky. Excelsior, sir.

SUMMER BLOCKBUSTERS AREN'T WHAT THEY USED TO BE

May 2007

I don't go to the movies much. The last film I saw in a theater was *The Hulk* (2003). It was awful. But it doesn't appear I'm missing much. This year's crop of summer blockbusters looks like another bunch of stinkers.

The current top three movies at the box office are all "threequels", the third installment in a series of franchise films; *Shrek, Spiderman,* and *Pirates of the Caribbean*, based on classic fairy tales, a classic comic book character, and a ride at Disney World, respectively. Coming soon are more franchise installments from *The Fantastic Four* and *Ocean's Thirteen*. When will they stop making sequels of movies that weren't very good to begin with? I'm fearful *The Simpson's Movie* will flop, blemishing the legacy of an otherwise landmark television show. When will Hollywood learn that movies made from television shows are always lousy? *Star Trek II: The Wrath of Khan* aside, can you think of one that was ever any good? *Charlie's Angels? Mission Impossible? The Brady Bunch?* Feh! We can look forward to feature-length theatrical versions of *24* an *I Dream of Jeanie* in 2008. Somebody pull the plug! Did *The X-Files Movie* teach us nothing? *The Beverly Hillbillies? The Flintstones? Scooby-Doo? The Dukes of Hazzard?* Make it stop! Make it stop!

But nostalgia makes cash registers ring. Familiar characters in stock stories are an easy sell to short attention span moviegoers. Even if the product is inferior, you can merchandise the name alone. Which is exactly what is happening throughout the entertainment industry. It's why *Hairspray* and Disney musicals dominate Broadway, and the hottest concert tickets this summer are for *American Idols Live* and a reunion tour by The Police. Why be original when you can repackage a proven winner?

Which brings us to this column's original subject matter: the 30th anniversary of *Star Wars* (1977). *Star Wars* is said to be the first great summer blockbuster, though *Jaws* (1975) should really get the credit. But there's no denying *Star Wars'* cultural impact. It's a great film; even 30 years after its release, it holds up as fast-paced, swashbuckling fun. Yes, the *Star Wars* franchise has yielded such unforgivable merchandising atrocities as the Ewoks and Jar Jar Binks, but that first film is a timeless classic. Plus it has the rare distinction of spawning a sequel, *The Empire Strikes Back*, which equals, if not surpasses, the original. This puts it in the elite company of such films as *Godfather 2*, *Aliens*, and *Evil Dead 2*.

Getting nostalgic about *Star Wars* is a bit ironic since the film itself is a nostalgia piece encompassing George Lucas' love of old Hollywood westerns, Buck Rogers-type space operas, and Akira Kurosawa's *The Hidden Fortress*. But Lucas used nostalgia to create a unique cinematic vision.

If Lucas were starting out in Hollywood today, some pinhead producer would tell him to shelf his script and focus on making a big screen version of *The Lone Ranger* or maybe a remake of *Forbidden Planet* or *Flash Gordon*.

It's this lack of original artistic effort that's turned the summer blockbuster into a field of stale, merchandise-driven commodities. It's one of the reasons—right behind a lack of funds, lack of time, and a lack of babysitters—that I don't go to the movies much anymore. Ah well, maybe I'll get out next year, when the sequel to *The Hulk* comes out…

They've all made it to the big screen now. Hulk. Iron Man. Wolverine. Thor. Even Doctor Strange. All of the superheroes I followed growing up are movie stars now.

So why don't I care? Why did I fall asleep during the last three Star Wars *movies? These films should touch all the warm and fuzzy spots in my childhood memories, but they don't. Maybe it's because I see the contrivance, I know what the creators of the Marvel cinematic universe are up to, and I won't give myself over to it, won't allow myself to enjoy the simple nostalgic fun. Or maybe superhero movies are just loud, flashy, and shitty.*

I've grown old, but I'm pretty sure I haven't grown up. You know you're old when the entertainment you grew up with is repackaged to sell cars and cola…and Broadway tickets…

Rob Errera

SPIDERMAN MUSICAL THE LATEST BROADWAY JOKE

I saw the signs go up outside the Foxwoods Theater on 42nd Street a year ago and thought it was a joke.

Spiderman: Turn Off The Dark with music and lyrics by Bono and The Edge from U2.

I went through the typical stages of grief: denial, anger, bargaining, and depression. But I had to accept it. Spidey, beloved comic book icon, would be singing and dancing on the Great White Way. WTF?

Economics drive Broadway theater (as it does so many things) and nostalgia sells. Broadway has always catered to older white couples, the demographic with the most money. Now I fall into that demographic (minus the money) and Broadway is packed with shows that mine the memories of my childhood. *The Addams Family Musical. Mary Poppins. Wicked. Jersey Boys. Mamma Mia. American Idiot,* featuring the music of Green Day. A stinking dung heap called *Rock of Ages* ("featuring the music of Journey, Styx, and REO Speedwagon!"). A revival of *The Pee Wee Herman Show*.

(The Pee Wee show actually looks kinda fun, probably because it originated as live theater, and isn't ripping off another artistic format.)

You can predict the Broadway line-up of 2020 based on today's pop culture dreck; *Facebook The Musical, Bad Romance featuring the music of Lady Gaga, Survivor the Musical, The Jersey Shore Live.* If you think Broadway can't get any more lame, it will.

Modern theater is far removed from its origins in ancient Greece, when Sophocles, Aeschylus, Aristophanes, and Euripides wrote plays about the corruption of power, the importance of family, the challenges of parenting, and the complications of romantic love. These are the same themes that drive primetime dramas and sitcoms today; Greek playwrights gave them dramatic form 2,500 years ago (all while adhering to a strict poetic structure, no less).

Broadway today is a snake eating its own tail, a pop culture monster consuming itself. Once upon a time, original Broadway musicals and plays were made into movies (*Showboat, The Sound Of Music, Guys and Dolls, West Side Story*). Now Hollywood blockbusters, regardless of artistic merit, are being adapted for Broadway (*Elf: The Musical*). Instead of building on the literary and theatrical foundations laid by William Shakespeare, Eugene O'Neill, and Tennessee Williams, Broadway is trying to compete with action movies and video games, complete with computer-generated imagery, special effects, chase scenes and explosions. I'm surprised the Theater District Ad Council hasn't adopted the slogan "Broadway: The Original 3-D Experience!"

Things are going in the wrong direction, as Broadway tries to steal market share from Imax theaters and multiplexes. The result is *Spiderman: Turn Off The Dark*, which, at $65 million, is the most expensive musical ever produced. It's apparently one of the most dangerous, too. Several performers were hurt, one seriously, while performing the show's high-flying stunts. But Spidey tickets are selling well, though I suspect the crowds are a lot like NASCAR fans—half show up expecting to see an accident.

Modern theater is a money-driven popularity contest…and maybe that's not so different from ancient times.

The Greeks were a competitive bunch (they started the Olympics, too) and their playwriting festivals would pit one performance against another, with the crowd favorite getting a coveted prize (accolades and a wreath of ivy). Plays often featured the "celebrities" of the time, religious and political leaders and their families. In a way, Sophocles' *Oedipus Rex*, was the *American Idol* winner of its day, the most popular performance that season.

Popular theater continues to reflect the needs and interest of the masses. Give the people what they want. The ancient Greeks understood that. It's the culture that feeds and fuels Broadway that's gotten trashy.

Broadway theater is currently fueled by Disney films, Spongebob Squarepants, *and a Bruce Springsteen residency. Original plays and musicals are being produced somewhere, but it's not on The Great White Way. Disney owns everything…and it's rewriting history (and myth) to suit its needs.*

HERCULES: DISNEY HAPPILY REWRITES HISTORY

October 1996

It's time to tell the ugly truth about Disneyfication.

I became aware of Disneyfication while baby-sitting a three-year-old boy. As a responsible baby-sitter, I immediately asked the child if he'd like to watch a movie until bedtime. His choice was Disney's version of *Hercules*.

The animation and voices were up to Disney's usual high standards. I was particularly impressed with the seamless blending of computer-generated graphics and old-school animation cels. But something in the story didn't sit quite right with me. This wasn't the legend of Hercules I learned in grade-school and studied in college.

Disney's *Hercules* kicks off with baby Hercules being cradled by his loving parents, Zeus and Hera. But according to Greek myth, Zeus descended from Mount Olympus and assumed the shape of the mortal Amphitryon and seduced

31

Amphitryon's wife, Alcmene. From this illicit union, Hercules is born. Hera resents Hercules since he's a constant reminder of her husband's infidelities.

At first I figure, hey, it's a kid's movie and Disney wants to portray wholesome family values. I'm okay with that. But then they introduce Megara, Hercules' love interest. Disney's love story spans beyond the realms of death and back. While heartwarming, it's completely inaccurate.

The way the Greeks tell it, Megara was a "trophy wife" bestowed upon Hercules after he defended Thebes against Orchomenus. Though they had several children together, Herc and Meg had an unhappy marriage. Things took a real downward turn when Hera (Herc's loving mother, remember?) sends Lyssa, the Fury of madness, to visit Hercules. The musclehead goes berserk, takes an ax, and chops up Meg and the kids. There goes Disney's G-rating! When the spell of madness wears off, Hercules is forced to flee the country and complete The Twelve Labors as penance for his crimes.

There's endless reconstruction of Greek myth in Disney's *Hercules*, too much to chronicle here. (Okay, just one more: In Disney's tale, Hercules travels to the underworld to save Meg from the evil clutches of Hades. But according to legend, Herc's trip to hell was actually the last of The Twelve Labors. Hercules was ordered to go to the underworld and fetch Cerberus, the monster-dog guardian of the infernal gates. Hercules, of course, promptly whips that puppy into shape, kicking Hades' butt along the way.) As entertaining and innocuous as Disney's version of Hercules may be, it is inaccurate. And that bothers me.

Disney has a fool-proof formula; take a name-recognition story and make a happy cartoon out of it. This worked fine when Disney remade classic fairy tales like "Snow White" and "Sleeping Beauty." But Disney has crossed the line between entertainment and alternate history. They trivialized Victor Hugo's *The Hunchback of Notre Dame* and botched the Native American legend of Pocahontas.

When Oliver Stone rewrites history for cinematic effect, as in *JFK* and *Nixon*, every one is up in arms. But Oliver Stone makes films for adults who are hopefully intelligent enough to recognize when he's bending the truth for dramatic effect. How is a kid supposed to know what they're seeing isn't true? Who is Disney to spoon-feed children misinformation about historical events and cultural heritage? Where will Disney's "happy paintbrush" strike next? *Roots* without slavery? *The Holocaust* without slaughter? *The Michael Jackson Story* without plastic surgery and child-abuse allegations?

If you learn anything from this lesson in Disneyfication, learn this—I probably shouldn't be asked to baby-sit.

I wrote this six years before becoming a father. Now my kids are teenagers, and old enough to understand why Hercules chopped up his family.

CLASSIC COMICS: PARTING WITH A PIECE OF AMERICAN HISTORY

April 2007

Of the dozen old comic books I had for sale on Ebay, I'd only miss one: *Crime SuspenStories #22*. It had a classic cover by artist Johnny Craig: a mid-level shot of a man holding a dripping ax in one hand, and a woman's severed head in the other. The woman's eyes are rolled up white, mouth hanging open, her feet visible on the floor behind her. It's an arresting image, even by today's ultra-violent standards. When it was first published in April 1954 it made an indelible mark on American culture.

America in the 1950s was a time of Cold War paranoia. The United States government drafted up lists of suspected communists and tried to figure out ways to save America's youth from the perils of rock 'n' roll music and comic books. A media-savvy psychiatrist (think Dr. Phil of the '50s) named Dr. Fredric Wertham published a book called *Seduction of the Innocent* that blamed comic books for all manner of juvenile delinquency. Wertham's sensational book prompted a Congressional hearing on juvenile delinquency that scrutinized sex and violence in comic books. The cover of *Crime SuspenStories #22* was frequently cited, as were the covers and images from *Tales From The Crypt*, EC's flagship horror title.

EC Comics publisher William Gaines sensed impending government censorship in the comic book industry and worked to prevent it. He urged his fellow publishers to police themselves and soon the Comics Magazine Association of America and its Comics Code Authority were born. Wholesalers wouldn't carry titles unless they had the CCA stamp of approval, which meant the comic books were reviewed for objectionable content. The CCA stamp is still in use, though it doesn't carry the clout it once did; hundreds of modern comic books are widely distributed today without the CCA stamp.

William Gaines ultimately found the CCA's guidelines too restrictive and left the group he helped create. By the mid-1950s, government scrutiny and bad press killed the sales of his once-successful horror and crime comics. The only EC Comic to survive was one that parodied his earlier horror titles called *Tales Calculated to Drive You Mad*. A short time later he changed the comic book to magazine size and simplified the title to *Mad Magazine*, which became one of the most enduring humor and satire publications in history. Gaines' story had a happy ending after all.

The copy of *Crime SuspenStories #22* I owned was in rough condition but it had a rich history. I kept a bunch of other old EC Comics —maybe I should keep this one too? I asked my wife's opinion as I outlined the history for her. She grimaced when I showed her the cover.

"Do you really think I should sell it?" I asked.

"Duh," she said. "Yeah."

Clearly, she didn't share my appreciation for this comic book's storied place in American literary history. I wasn't sure anyone else would either. We live in a time when terrorist videos of actual beheadings are all too common. Is there even a market for an old, beat-up comic book notable for its beheading cover?

I'm pleased to report there was. Nearly 20 people watched my auction, 14 bids were placed, and the guy who won paid nearly twice what I thought it was worth. It's good to know I'm not the only warped person out there with an appreciation for severed heads.

I don't think it made my wife feel any better, though...

My wife doesn't share my love of graphic comic books or horror films, but her love of true crime is boundless. My wife likes to keep it real...maybe a little too real. Now I'm scared.

ZEN AND THE ART OF THE ADULT COLORING BOOK

June 2015

Remember *The Secret Garden*? No, not that stodgy English children's tale. The adult coloring book!

I'm talking about a grab-your-crayons-and-find-a-sunny-place-to-work kind of coloring book. Adult coloring books are hot sellers around the globe, and *The Secret Garden* recently topped the New York Times Bestseller list. French publisher Hachette has a collection called *Art-Thérapie* with twenty volumes including all kinds of drawings, from butterflies and flowers, to cupcakes, graffiti, and psychedelic patterns. In the United Kingdom, illustrator Mel Simone Elliot's *Colour Me Good* series lets you color-in pictures of celebrities like Ryan Gosling, Lady Gaga, Beyonce, and Kate Moss. Spanish cartoonist Antonio Fraguas, or Forges, published *Coloréitor*, "a de-stress book."

Grown-up coloring books are marketed as a way to escape the media bombardment of the digital world and rediscover the do-it-yourself joys of something simple and stress-free.

According to psychologists, coloring activates both halves of the brain, stimulating creative skills as well as a sense of logic and reason. Coloring can bring a sense of relaxation that lowers activity in the amygdala, the part of the brain that controls emotion and is affected by stress.

One of the most common symbols found in adult coloring books are mandalas, spiritual symbols from India that represent the universe. Mandalas have circular designs with concentric shapes and geometric symmetry, like the intricate patterns of a flower. One of the first psychologists to use coloring mandalas as a relaxation technique was Carl G. Jüng in the early 20th century.

The first time I saw an adult using a coloring book was during an early episode of the reality show *The Osbournes* back in 2002. Here was Ozzy Osbourne, the Dark Prince of Rock 'n' Roll, sitting at his kitchen table, surrounded by foul-mouthed chaos, calmly working a color-by-number landscape with a package of Magic Markers. He looked like an overgrown child, carefully selecting each color, and staying within the lines. The Ozzman was way ahead of the unwinding-through-art curve.

The Zen-like instructions for one of Amazon's bestselling adult coloring books tells the story:

1. Break out your crayons or colored pencils.

2. Turn off your phone, tablet, computer, whatever.

3. Stop thinking about your job, your credit score, your reputation with your co-workers, your goals, your waistline, your retirement savings, etc.

4. Remind yourself that coloring is like dancing, or being alive. It doesn't have a point; it *is* the point.

5. Find your favorite page in the book. That is the beginning.

6. Start coloring.

7. If you notice at any point that you are having fun, forgetting your worries, daydreaming freely, feeling more creative, excitable, curious, delighted, relaxed or any combination thereof, breathe deeply and take a moment to enjoy it. Then, gently return your attention to coloring.

8. When you are satisfied or don't feel like it anymore, stop.

Adult coloring books are a way to recapture the innocence of youth. They also give artists a sense of control; everything's got a specific shape and color, just follow the key and stay in the lines. Color-by-number and fill-in-the-blank style artwork offers a "shortcut" for artists of all skill levels. You can create your own artistic masterpiece without the talent and/or training of a fine artist!

Pablo Picasso said, "Art washes away from the soul the dust of everyday life." This is why adult coloring books are so popular. They cleanse the soul, or at least give your mind and spirit a rest, a chance to create something colorful, pretty, and uniquely your own.

Plus, it's good to get your fingers working something besides a keyboard, touch screen, or remote control for a change.

Find your inner artist…and nurture it!

COOKIE MONSTER GETS AN EXTREME MAKE-OVER

April 2005

When it comes to children's television, *Sesame Street* is one of the best. Disney's stuff is too slick and processed for my liking. The Wiggles make me uncomfortable in a "Michael Jackson slumber party" sort of way. The Teletubbies and Boo-Bah are simply freaky-weird.

But I have to question *Sesame Street*'s decision to give Cookie Monster a personality make-over. *Sesame Street* kicked off its 35th season by promoting a healthier lifestyle for children. With childhood obesity rates soaring, they want to make sure kids learn the importance of healthy eating habits and exercise. The first step toward accomplishing this goal is teaching Cookie Monster that cookies are a "sometimes food" only enjoyed on occasion. In fact, Cookie's signature song, "C Is For Cookie" will be replaced by a new number, "Cookie Is A Sometimes Food."

Sesame Street should show children the results of obesity and excessive cookie eating first-hand. Have Cookie ask a girl out on a date and get turned down because he's too fat. Or have Cookie go on a job interview and not get the gig because he's got chocolate chip crumbs scattered all over his blue fur.

Maybe he has nothing to wear to the Monster Parade because none of his clothes fit anymore. Or perhaps he's heading down to Hooper's Store with Big Bird and Snuffleupagus and keels over of a heart attack. Have Cookie lose a furry blue leg to diabetes. This is the reality of obesity. Why sugar coat it, so to speak?

I'm not against teaching kids healthy eating habits (I wish someone had taught me when I was a kid) or showing people (or monsters) change for the better, but I question changing such a fundamental personality trait of a beloved character like Cookie Monster. Part of the magic of *Sesame Street*, part of what makes it so appealing to children and adults alike, is the residents of *Sesame Street* are so human…even the monsters. Snuffy has low self-esteem. Grover has delusions of grandeur. Oscar needs an anger management class. The Count's number fixation borders on an obsessive-compulsive disorder. In short, all of the *Sesame Street* characters are flawed in some way (I wish Elmo would stop referring to himself in the third person—" Elmo loves you!").

But the people, monsters, and muppets of *Sesame Street* accept each other for who they are, flaws, quirks, and all. It doesn't matter if you're an eight-foot yellow bird or a short, fat, furry monster—there's room for everyone on *Sesame Street*. These lessons of tolerance and acceptance are most important. I hope the *Sesame Street* executives don't lose sight of them when they make over Cookie Monster.

A Cookie Monster makeover? What's next? A trashy Barbie doll?

BARBIE TOPPLED BY TOY TARTS

March 2006

Toys-R-Us was crowded, screaming kids running everywhere, and I had reached the limit of my patience. My two-year-old daughter, Francesca, was raring to go, pointing wildly at a display of dolls.

"Doll!" she screamed. "Baby doll!"

I looked at what she wanted. It was a display of Barbie-like dolls called "Bratz." They could have just as easily been called "Slutz." These dolls looked frighteningly similar to the streetwalkers who used to mill around the Greyhound bus terminal in Manhattan. Their hair was long and ridiculously luxurious (extensions, no doubt), tight clothes hugged overly curvy figures, except for the tiny midriff which was provocatively bare. They stood on giant platform heels, flashy jewelry ("bling") dangling from their ears, necks, wrists, and fingers. Heavy eye make-up and dark lipstick completed the "inner city 'ho" look.

I did a double take. These dolls looked like something you'd find in an adult novelty store. Why were they being marketed toward children? Next to the Bratz display, was a collection of "Baby Bratz." Imagine a doll designed to look like a baby girl, only with the same obscene hair, make-up, and jewelry as the bigger Bratz. These babies wore tiny "diaper hot pants," revealing belly shirts, and carried their baby bottles on metal chains slung over their shoulders. The "baby slut" look was sickeningly complete. Just like those demented child beauty pageants, these dolls were blatantly sexualizing little children. What the !@#$?

"Doll!" Francesca yelled again.

"No," I told her. "You can't have one of those. Your doll is in the car and we'll be finished here in a minute."

This wasn't the answer Francesca wanted. She started throwing a tantrum. A bloated and inappropriately dressed group of Mommies hanging around the Bratz display (who, in fact, looked like grown-up-and-gone-to-seed versions of the Bratz dolls themselves) gave me the hairy eyeball. Don't be so uptight, the look said, just buy your kid a doll if she wants one.

Barbie was once considered a bad role model for little girls. It's true, Barbie's long legs, tiny waist, big chest, and mane of long blonde hair certainly represents an unrealistic role model for most young girls. That's why Mattel went to great lengths some years ago trying to smarten Barbie up with the "Doctor Barbie" and "Banker Barbie" playsets. She still had a killer bod, but at least she now had professional career aspirations.

Today Barbie looks like a choir-girl compared to the Bratz babes. Their aspirations are less lofty than Barbie's; featured among the Bratz collection is All-Night Mall Party, Sushi Bar, and Stylin' Salon 'N' Spa. Whereas Barbie always looks like she's ready for a day at the beach (even Doctor Barbie looks like she'd rather be surfing), the Bratz dolls look like

43

they just stepped out of a hip-hop video. They look ready to kick Barbie's ass and steal the keys to her convertible.

But despite their questionable image, the Bratz dolls are top sellers. Many credit the dolls' success to the fact that they bring a hip, modern, multi-ethnic sensibility to the bland children's toy market.

"Girls wanted dolls that emulated their older sisters," says Murray Bass, CEO of Chic Boutique, Inc., a company that manufactures and distributes children's toys. "What Mattel was offering at the time wasn't what was out there in the real world. Bratz had the look."

But is this "the look" we want our children emulating? I'm all for celebrating cultural diversity, but why does that translate to children presented as sex objects? How can we expect the next generation of American women to aspire to be anything but trashy 'hos when we give them Paris Hilton and Bratz dolls as role models when they are young?

By some small miracle, Francesca and I made it out of Toys R Us and back to the car. Her doll was waiting for her, as promised. Baby Doll, an unassuming purple doll with a plastic face and a soft body, looked a little thread-bare after two years of hard use, but I figured she had a couple more good years left in her. I hoped so—I shuddered to think of who, or what, might replace her.

The Bratz hit their peak in 2007 with the release of The Bratz Movie, *but slumping sales and copyright lawsuits have all but leveled the Bratz brand, though it did relaunch in Fall 2018. Barbie continues to limp along, awaiting her rebirth as an iconic American brand. Everything old is new again in time…except for Toys R Us.*

Beware of clumsily assembled nostalgia.

STRANGER THINGS TOYS WITH YOUR MEMORIES AND PUTS THEM AWAY SOILED

February 2017

Spoiler alert: The Netflix original series *Stranger Things* may ruin once-pleasant childhood memories.

Despite strong critical acclaim for *Stranger Things* (the series picked up a slew of honors at the recent Screen Actor's Guild Awards) I had a bad, visceral reaction to this sci-fi/horror series, specifically with the clumsy and thoughtless way writers/directors/producers, the Duffer Brothers, attempted to recreate classic moments from '80s creature features.

There are bright spots in *Stranger Things*. The series features several fine young actors who deliver astonishingly mature and nuanced performances. Millie Bobby Brown, Finn Wolfhard, Gaten Matarazzo, Noah Schapp, and Caleb McLaughlin are the stars of tomorrow, and it's nice to see '80s icon Winona Ryder back in fine form. *Stranger Things* does an outstanding job of channeling an '80s vibe. The sets, costuming, styling, and music are all spot on.

The problem is the Duffer Brothers get so bogged down recreating their favorite '80s movies moments, they forget to tell a story of their own. The Duffers take the cheesiest clichés from the most heavy-handed movies of the 1980s and reproduce them verbatim. Scenes and scenarios are lifted directly from *Halloween, Aliens, Poltergeist*, and *ET,* while the synth-heavy score sounds like a John Carpenter or Dario Argento outtake.

Stranger Things looks nice, but there's nothing new, exciting, or interesting here. Even casual horror fans will be able to predict plot twists, dialogue, and even camera angles with a high level of accuracy. *Stranger Things* ultimately devolves into campy horror that tries to pay homage to H.P. Lovecraft and *The Evil Dead* but can't get past its own ham-fisted storytelling. *Stranger Things* takes itself too seriously, offering the lurid and ludicrous situations of grindhouse films without the absurdity that make such movies palatable and fun.

Stranger Things owes its existence to the success of Ryan Murphy and Brad Falchuk's horror series for FX, *American Horror Story.* Murphy and Falchuk look at the horror genre as a whole, and find links between Lon Chaney's silent films and *Paranormal Experience*, between Tod Browning's disturbing classic *Freaks* and Stephen King's nightmarish clowns, and tell *new* tales of terror with the building blocks of classic horror. The Duffer Brothers never make it out of the '80s aisle at Blockbuster, hacking together a narrow-focused, "Best-Of-1980s-Horror" compilation that might be well liked on YouTube, but has no place passing as "award-winning original entertainment."

The success of *Stranger Things* is confounding and annoying. It takes a brilliant, ground-breaking concept and makes it worse. It doesn't improve or add to the genre it so dearly loves, only exploits it. And the popularity of this show means it will spawn even more nostalgia-raping dreck. *American Horror Story* begat *Stranger Things*, but it's de-evolution, a misguided backwards step, like watching prehistoric man douse his fire and climb back into the trees.

The Duffer Brothers broke into the part of my mind where I store my memories of classic '80s horror films, played roughly with everything, and put stuff back askew and smudged with peanut butter and jelly fingerprints. I felt personally violated by *Stranger Things*…and that's a strange thing, indeed.

I've got a big bug up my ass about Stranger Things, *and it drives my wife and daughter nuts. "It's a great show! Why can't Dad chill out and just enjoy it?" They're probably right; I expect too much from my mindless entertainment. But "chill out and just enjoy it" sounds like something a molester whispers to a victim. The Duffer Brothers have touched my mind and memories in a Bad Place.*

ABE LINCOLN: VAMPIRE HUNTER
AND OTHER DUMB IDEAS

June 2012

We live in confusing times. If you're like many modern Americans, you're perplexed and haunted by one burning question: What the hell is *Abraham Lincoln: Vampire Hunter* all about?

The idea seems so…so…stupid. And you're right. It *is* stupid. I have no idea why *Abraham Lincoln: Vampire Hunter* was made into a major motion picture. But I *can* tell you where this stupid idea originated.

A new literary subgenre emerged in 2009 when author Seth Grahame-Smith published the monster mash-up, *Pride And Prejudice and Zombies*. Jane Austen's classic novel of English manners is given a modern update with the inclusion of flesh-eating adversaries and ninjas.

Seth Grahame-Smith's entertaining novel was a surprise hit. A bunch of similar monster mash-ups followed, including

Sense and Sensibility and Sea Monsters, The Adventures of Huckleberry Finn and Zombie Jim, The Undead World of Oz, and *Alice in Zombieland.* Seth Grahame-Smith's follow-up novel, *Abraham Lincoln: Vampire Hunter,* expanded the boundaries of this weird genre even further by including historical fiction in the monster mash-up.

Why was Honest Abe the first to make it to the big screen? Beats me. From what I hear, *Pride and Prejudice And Zombies* will be shambling into theaters before long. Maybe *AL:VH's* producers thought it would be interesting to see the president who ended slavery battle vampires during an election year when the first black president is running for re-election. One of the plot points in *Abraham Lincoln: Vampire Hunter* is that most slave owners are vampires looking for an easy source of fresh blood. The producers are banking on the hope that America will embrace this odd blend of American history and bloodsuckers.

And why not? Sure, *Abraham Lincoln: Vampire Hunter* is a stupid idea. So are lots of things. *Buffy, the Vampire Slayer*—about a high school cheerleader who kills bloodsuckers—is a pretty dumb idea too, but Joss Whedon turned it into a brilliantly executed, campy television series.

The entire monster mash-up literary genre is a dumb idea. But that doesn't mean it can't get a foothold in the public consciousness and become popular. If pop history has shown us anything, it's that the public loves a stupid idea.

I wish the makers of *Abraham Lincoln: Vampire Hunter* all the best. Looks like they're going to need it based on the opening weekend box office. I'll be surprised if Honest Abe isn't already on his way to DVD. Personally, I think this genre needs to mature a bit. I'm waiting for *Ronald Reagan vs. Godzilla,* or *A Nightmare On Occupy Wall Street.*

I love horror films. As a weird, eccentric teen I sought out obscure horror films with my weird, eccentric friends. Good horror was hard to find. Now the most popular show on television is about flesh-eating zombies. Gore is hot, but not as cool as it used to be. Good horror is still hard to find.

MAINSTREAMING OF GORE MAKES BLOOD RUN COLD

October 2013

Everybody loves a zombie.

Flesh-eating ghouls are all the rage, featured in popular television shows like *The Walking Dead*, and books/films like *World War Z*.

For years, vampires were the teacher's pet of the monster class. You can trace the appeal of the vampire's cool, sophisticated charm from *Dracula*, to *Interview With A Vampire*, to *Twilight*.

But zombies have risen up to become the hot monster of the moment. People identify with the mindless drive and determination of zombies. Their relentless need to consume is all-American, as is their never-say-die attitude.

My love affair with zombies goes back to childhood, watching George Romero's *Night of the Living Dead* with my father on The Late Show.

During my teenage years, I enjoyed Sex and Violence Nights with my friends. We'd rent two videos—one naughty, one nasty—and pig out on pizza and junk food while we watched. The sex videos were fairly tame—usually a Russ Meyer breast-fest or something featuring sorority cheerleaders.

But the violent videos were hardcore. We craved gore, and we'd search far and wide for the most extreme stuff we could find. We discovered Hershell Gordon Lewis's *The Wizard of Gore* and *Blood Feast*. We basked in the low-budget badness of *Basket Case, Bloodsucking Freaks*, and hundreds of other blood-splattered B-films.

Our quest for cinematic grossness introduced us to sub-titled terrors by a slew of foreign filmmakers: Lamberto Bava, Dario Argento, Lucio Fulci. One of my favorite zombie scenes is an underwater fight sequence between a shark and a zombie in Fulci's *Zombie*! (*Zombi2*). It's a feat of mindboggling cinematography that holds up to this day— and should inspire a SyFy original movie by next summer. ("From the people who brought you *Sharknado* and *Sharktopus—Zombark*!")

Watching hardcore horror was what young geeks did in the 1980s. My friends and I were not alone. Lots of people grew up with violent entertainment. As a result, the once-rare, formerly taboo thrills of splatter flicks have made their way to primetime television courtesy of AMC's zombie-fest, *The Walking Dead*.

The Walking Dead drew 16.1 million viewers in its season four debut, rivaling TV's most watched shows—*The Big Bang Theory* and *NCIS*. Those numbers may be even bigger when *The Walking Dead* returns from its mid-season break. In fact, *The Walking Dead* is pulling in more viewers in the coveted 18-49 demographic than professional football games.

Each episode of *TWD* features enough gore and violence to rival any Fulci or Romero film. Decapitations, spilling guts, and bloody bites are the backbone of zombie horror, and *TWD* revels in the gruesome traditions of Grand Guignol.

Aside from cartoonish violence, *TWD* also delivers scenes of harrowing psychological terror. There's not much time to grieve lost loved ones on *The Walking Dead*; you have to crush their skulls before they reanimate and eat you. Everyone's infected, the threat of death is constant, and the future is bleak.

As much as I love *TWD*, its popularity is somewhat freakish. My friends and I had to seek this stuff out when we were teenagers, special-ordering it from Mom and Pop video stores. We had to *work* to feed our weird interests.

Nobody has to work hard to find violent visuals anymore. Graphic images of every sort are a mere click away, scalable to your computer, tablet, or smartphone. Everything's too easy. Broadband makes us lazy, desensitized, and numb.

Gore-hounds were once a small sub-culture of the cult movie circuit. Now we're everywhere. Millions of others share my twisted bloodlust.

And that makes it less fun.

Groucho Marx said he didn't want to belong to any club that would have him as a member. I feel the same about the normalization of gore. Maybe becoming a parent changed me, or maybe I've simply gotten old. But I liked it better when you had to *work* to be weird. Graphic images— whether violent or sexual—should be harder to find. Do some digging if that's what you want to see. But bringing extreme violence and gore into mainstream entertainment makes my blood run cold.

Rob Errera

I sound like a prude, but TV and movies need less blood and better writing. Maybe I'm just disappointed with the downward turn The Walking Dead *has taken. Anybody still hate-watching that POS?*

INSIDE AMERICA'S ZOMBIE LOVE AFFAIR

October 2015

With Halloween right around the corner and a new season of the hit TV-series *The Walking Dead* underway, now is a good time to address America's love affair with zombies.

Prior to George Romero's 1968 horror classic, *The Night of the Living Dead*, zombies were only seen in a handful of B-movies about Haitian voodoo. Voodoo zombies were corpses resurrected through black magic, undead henchmen that did the bidding of a voodoo priest or priestess.

Romero's zombies were a reflection of modern society. Romero's zombies looked and dressed like "Average Joes." Half the fun of zombie entertainment is spotting "on-the-job zombies"—zombie cheerleader, zombie policemen, zombie nurse, etc. Zombies were once regular people with regular jobs before transforming into flesh-eating monsters. Only a heartbeat keeps you from turning into one of them. That might be the scariest aspect of zombie-dom; the idea of losing who you are and being (literally) swallowed by, and assimilated into, a mindless mob.

Zombies are like us in so many ways, for example:

Zombies love to eat. Who doesn't? Three-quarters of Americans are overweight. An even higher percentage is addicted to sugar. Both the living and the walking dead are highly food motivated.

Zombies are creatures of habit. They do the same things over and over again, which anyone with a tedious job can relate to. They return to places they frequented when they were alive, which is one of the reasons why Romero's second zombie flick, *Dawn of the Dead*, is set in a shopping mall filled with shambling, flesh-eating corpses. Zombies are the ultimate consumers.

Zombies are driven, determined, and never-say-die. They keep on going and going, like the Energizer Bunny with a taste for human flesh. You have to admire the tenacity of zombies. They've got guts, and they're not afraid to spill 'em.

Zombies fall apart. They remind us of our own mortality. Many of us feel the aches and pains of aging and we relate to the frail physicality of a rotting corpse. Zombies are grim reminders of the weakness and limitations of our own skin.

Zombies are terrifying because they multiply and swarm like cockroaches or rats. All zombie tales become a math-class word problem with humanity on the losing end of the equation. Zombies spread exponentially, man! It's Zombageddon!

What causes a zombie apocalypse? Romero suggested a passing comet or meteor caused the dead to rise and eat the living. Modern zombie plagues are often linked to a "mutant virus," which reflects our immune-deficient society's fear of sickness and disease. Other storytellers have combined the two philosophies and blame the zombie apocalypse on "a mutant virus from outer space."

But every zombie apocalypse is created by writers and directors, readers and viewers, who can't resist the thrills, chills, and metaphoric opportunities zombie tales offer.

What would Holden Caulfield make of America's love affair with zombies? I think he'd understand.

DIGITIZE SALINGER AND OTHER LITERARY PURSUITS

April 2014

I went through a "Why Didn't I Read This in High School?" phase recently, and J.D. Salinger's *The Catcher in the Rye* came up next on my reading list.

I was eager to download a copy of Salinger's classic novel onto my Kindle. I'm a firm backer of the digital publishing revolution, since ebooks let you:

1. Change the size and style of the text.

2. Look up word definitions and background info on the spot.

3. Highlight, makes notes, and export chunks of text.

These features are incredibly helpful when I'm writing book reviews (*bobsbookblog.com*), and must be a major timesaver for students working on school essays. (Back in my day, we had to write out notes and quotes by hand on index cards, whippersnappers!)

But *The Catcher in the Rye* isn't available on Kindle. You can't get it on your Nook or iPad either. J.D. Salinger never allowed any other editions of his novel other than the one published by Little, Brown and Company in 1951. The breakout success of *The Catcher in the Rye* spooked Salinger, and he retreated to his rural Vermont home after the book's publication. Salinger produced three additional books, but didn't publish again after 1961.

Salinger died in 2010, but his estate still closely guards the copyright on his work, never allowing any adaptations. Film directors from Elia Kazan to Steven Spielberg have been turned away, and the Salinger Estate still hasn't sanctioned audiobooks or digital editions.

If you want to read *The Catcher in the Rye* (or Salinger's other work) you have to order the same Little, Brown and Company mass market paperback (now in its 98th printing) that's been kicking around classrooms since forever. It's got the original 1951 orangey cover art by E. Michael Mitchell — an ink sketch of a carousel horse and the NYC skyline — on both the front and back. Besides the title and "a novel by J.D. Salinger," there is no other cover text, no sales copy, no About the Author copy, no blurbs from other authors or academics, and no "New York Times bestselling author." Nothing.

The interior of the book is equally sparse. There is no forward or afterword. No advertisements for other books, no offers to join Little, Brown and Company's Readers Club. There is no About the Author page here either. *The Catcher in the Rye* is 214 pages of Holden Caulfield's inimitably cranky narrative, presented exactly how the author intended, and it's been this way, unchanged, for nearly fifty years.

Salinger's over-protectiveness guarantees his work is uniformly consumed. I experienced *The Catcher in the Rye* the same way, in the same font and format, as nearly everyone else who ever read the book. I dog-eared pages, underlined in pencil, and scribbled notes in the margins, the same way lit students have for decades. Salinger's format constraints demand it.

According to a new documentary on J.D. Salinger, the late author left specific instructions for five books to be published between 2015 and 2020. I don't know what the Salinger Estate or Little, Brown and Company plan, but launching new Salinger titles is an ideal time to bring all the author's work into the digital realm. Contemporary literature should embrace contemporary formats, and ebooks are here to stay. Salinger's work needs to be readily available, brought into the digital realm, and forever preserved in binary code.

Digitize Salinger! And Harper Lee's *To Kill A Mockingbird*, too!

Update: You still can't buy a digital edition of The Catcher in the Rye *(though* To Kill A Mockingbird *is now available as an ebook). It makes me gonzo!*

GOOD NIGHT, GONZO PRINCE

February 2005

Hunter S. Thompson is dead, and the world of journalism says goodbye to one of its most unique voices.

Thompson's brand of "gonzo journalism" was at times reckless and irresponsible, but it was always funny and insightful. Like him or not, Hunter S. Thompson had a way with words.

I wish I could say I was a huge fan of Thompson's work, but I wasn't. He falls into my "Authors I Wish I Liked But Don't" category. This group includes several counter-culture icons, including Jack Kerouac, Henry Miller, and William S. Burroughs. I know it's cool and hip to like these edgy authors, but, for the most part, I was left unimpressed by their work.

I feel the same way about Hunter S. Thompson. He's written things that have made me laugh out loud, but mostly I find his writing style jarring, disjointed, and obscure. I guess this

61

works on some level as "concrete poetry"—reading his work sort of feels like tripping on the drugs he's describing—but it also makes for a tedious read. His personal appearances on talk shows were even more bizarre; he'd mumble and act strangely. I didn't get it.

Still, even though I'm not a big fan, Hunter Thompson was an inspiration of sorts. I was a confused college freshman majoring in biology when I first read *Fear And Loathing In Las Vegas*. My roommate, a journalism major, described it as "required reading". There are some hilarious moments in the book, but what struck me most about it was the freedom that came with being a writer. You could write about anything and everything. Hunter wasn't reporting about political conventions or motorcycle races, he was reporting about life itself, the world and his place in it, and the varying states of perception that define your reality.

Soon after reading Thompson's *Fear and Loathing* I stumbled upon another "required reading" book for aspiring journalists; Bob Woodward and Carl Bernstein's *All The President's Men*. The politics bored me, but I was drawn to the authors' dogged pursuit of the truth, another trait of a good reporter. Both Hunter S. Thompson and Woodward and Bernstein taught me that a journalist could write about anything—no matter how bizarre, no matter how sacred—as long as he was honest and got to the truth. Since I was a biology major who couldn't pass general biology, I switched majors to English with a focus on media and journalism.

And that, dear readers, is how Hunter S. Thompson helped plant the journalism seed for yours truly. If you think I'm clever and witty, then Hunter deserves partial credit. If you think I'm a hack then he's partially to blame. One thing is for sure, Hunter S. Thompson was a major influence on the world of journalism as a whole and on my career in particular.

I just wish I liked his stuff more…

I still can't find love for Hunter S. Thompson's prose. Vonnegut is more my style. I just wish I knew what Kurt was talking about…

VONNEGUT: DECIPHERING AN IDOL'S ADVICE

September 2005

There was an old guy wandering around the lobby of the office building where I worked. He looked vaguely familiar, but I didn't place him until the desk clerk called his name.

"Hey...aren't you Kurt Vonnegut?"

It *was* Kurt Vonnegut. He looked the same as he did on the back cover of my copy of *Slaughterhouse Five*. Only older, with wilder hair. The desk guy shook his hand. I did, too. "*Cat's Cradle* is one of my all-time favorites," I said. I wasn't lying.

A moment later the elevator doors opened and we both got on. I was alone in an elevator with one of my literary idols. I felt a little lightheaded, giddy, and nervous.

"Doing an interview with NPR today?" I asked. National Public Radio had studios on the seventh floor of our building.

"I hope so," Vonnegut said. "That's what they tell me."

An awkward pause followed. I kept staring at Vonnegut and I think it made him uncomfortable. He looked away and I stared at the numbers on the elevator panel. I knew I had roughly another minute before we reached the NPR floor. I cleared my throat and spoke.

"I do some fiction writing myself," I said.

"Yeah? What do you write?" Vonnegut asked.

"Science fiction. Mostly horror."

"You sell it?"

The question surprised me. Vonnegut judged writers the same way non-writers did. If their stuff didn't sell, they must not be very talented.

"I've sold a couple of things," I said. "Small press stuff." The most I'd been paid for a piece of fiction was fifty bucks. I won first place in a short story contest once. The prize was a plaque and ten copies of the magazine.

"Good for you," Vonnegut said, "Keep at it."

I had time to share one more thought.

"Writing is sort of a solitary profession, don't you think?"

Vonnegut laughed nervously, but he looked right at me and there was great sorrow in his gaze, and something else that looked like fear.

The elevator doors slid open.

"Stick with paperbacks," Vonnegut said as he stepped out. "That's all anyone ever reads these days."

I had no idea what Kurt Vonnegut was talking about. Maybe he was urging me to seek paperback publishers for my fiction. Maybe he was encouraging me to read more paperback novels. Maybe he was answering a question someone else had asked him hours before.

Instead of asking for clarification, I shouted, "Thanks!" as the elevator doors slid closed. Kurt Vonnegut was gone and I was alone again.

Ah, Kurt…I miss you. You, too, Mr. Crichton.

CRICHTON A MAN OF MANY HATS...AND IDEAS

November 2008

Life is full of ironies, and sometimes you don't have to look further than the front page of the newspaper to find them.

Michael Crichton died earlier this month after a brief battle with lung cancer. He was 66. Crichton was best known as the author of *Jurassic Park* and the creator of the TV series *ER*. While those are two of Crichton's most successful franchises, he displayed unique talents in a variety of other areas, too.

Crichton was a trained medical doctor and began writing and publishing novels under a pseudonym while in med school. It was the mid-'60s, and while many young men where getting stoned and listening to The Beatles (and/or fighting a war in Vietnam) Crichton took medical courses during the day and wrote medical thrillers by night. His 1968 novel, *A Case of Need* (written under the pen name Jeffery Hudson) won an Edgar Award in 1969 from the Mystery Writers of America.

In 1971, Crichton's novel, *The Andromeda Strain,* was made into a successful film by acclaimed director Robert Wise. Crichton himself began dabbling in film and before long he found himself behind the camera, writing and directing 1973's *Westworld* (featuring Yul Brynner as an out-of-control robo-cowboy) and directing 1978's *Coma.* Both films were popular thrillers in the 1970s.

Crichton continued to publish successful novels throughout the 1980s. He worked with Steven Spielberg on a film version of *ER* when Spielberg asked Crichton about his next project. Crichton said he was writing a novel about dinosaurs and DNA.

Spielberg was intrigued and back-burnered the *ER* project to work on Crichton's next piece, 1990's *Jurassic Park.* Crichton went on to write the sequel, 1995's *The Lost World*, and tweaked the script for *Jurassic Park III* (proving that not everything he touched turned to gold).

After the success of *Jurassic Park*, Spielberg and Crichton returned to the *ER* script, expanding it into a television series. They assembled a good ensemble of actors (including a handsome young buck named George Clooney) and the show was an instant hit. In late 1994 Crichton earned the unique distinction of having the #1 movie (*Jurassic Park*), the #1 TV show (*ER*), and the #1 book (*Disclosure*, atop the paperback list). Not bad for a guy taking time off from the doctorin' business.

The irony of Crichton's death is that it hit the news the same day scientists in Japan announced they had cloned mice from frozen DNA. It was previously believed that ice crystals would damage DNA, which was frozen for 16 years. But scientists used a new method to successfully replicate the DNA and produce cloned mice.

"This is the first time a mammal has been cloned from a sample stored at conditions reasonably close to what might be expected in permafrost," said scientist Teruhiko Wakayama, who led the study.

That means those frozen wooly mammoth and saber-tooth tiger carcasses that turn up in Siberia may someday walk the Earth again…or at least the confines of a zoo cage or theme park attraction. Crichton's *Jurassic Park*, a theme park filled with living dinosaurs, suddenly doesn't seem so fantastic an idea after all.

There is perhaps no bigger honor for a writer of science fiction than to see one of his/her far-fetched ideas become reality. Isaac Asimov saw his Three Laws of Robotics, which he published in 1942, put into practice by the robotics industry 20 years later. And Arthur C. Clarke saw communications satellites, which he wrote about in 1945, become tools for the everyday man.

Literary critics bash Crichton as a "formula writer" but he told good stories and he told them well. His ideas were as big as those of Asimov, Clarke, or Robert Heinlein. It's a shame he won't be around to see some of those big ideas come to pass. Though, in the case of *Jurassic Park*, maybe he's better off.

Love you, miss you, Mr. Crichton!

Rob Errera

HARRY POTTER AND THE PERISHING PUBLISHERS

November 2007

I don't know who Harry Potter is. I saw a few minutes of one of his movies once. Looked interesting…maybe I'll catch it from the beginning one day.

But I'll tell you something about Harry Potter—I love the guy! Harry Potter creator J.K. Rowling did what publishers thought impossible—she's gotten young people (indeed, readers of all ages, but young 'uns, for sure) interested in reading again. Not only reading, but reading fiction. And not only reading *fiction*, but reading *big, fat* works of fiction.

In the ADD Age, when all information has to be packaged in idiot-proof 30- or 60-second chunks, the Harry Potter phenomenon is a pleasant anomaly. For the world of book publishing it's a ray of hope in an otherwise bleak and dying landscape. Harry Potter aside, people aren't reading books anymore. An AP-Poll released recently showed that one-in-four adults didn't read any books at all last year. In 2004, a

70

National Endowment for the Arts report titled "Reading at Risk" found only 57 percent of American adults had read a book in 2002, a four percent drop in the last decade.

Books are the tip of the iceberg. Newspapers also face extinction. Fifty years ago newspapers were everybody's main source of news and information—now it's a last stop (if at all) after television, radio, and Google searches.

It's easy to blame television, movies, and the Internet for the decline of reading, but it's more than that. A love of reading is passed from parents to children. But as fewer parents read, so too do fewer children. Studies show the majority of readers are over 50. The big publishing news last week was that Margaret Mitchell's estate had licensed another *Gone With The Wind* book, this one told from Rhett Butler's perspective. What does that tell you about the median age of readers? Reading, especially reading for sheer enjoyment, is becoming a lost pastime. Which makes writers, from hacks like me, to bestsellers like Stephen King, an endangered species (gulp!).

I'm doing my part to keep the "reading arts" alive. I read a lot—close to 50 books a year not including magazines, and non-fiction titles. There's nothing better than losing yourself in a good book. And, for the money, it's still the best value in entertainment. An $8 paperback can entertain me for nearly a week; a $10 movie is over in two hours. Plus the special effects (and sex scenes) I conjure in my head are always better than anything Hollywood can produce.

My wife also does her part passing a love of reading on to our kids. Nothing makes my three-year-old daughter happier than a trip to the library. (She keeps taking out the same book, though—a technical manual about fire trucks complete with schematics and wiring diagrams. Hey, at least she's reading; "enjoying a book" might be a better description.) We read to both our kids before bed and, even

71

though children's books are light on text, heavy on pictures, we try to instill a sense of value about books and the words they contain. There are wonders, magic, and fun waiting on the pages of books—just crack one open and your journey begins.

Magic and wonder are certainly key ingredients to Harry Potter's success. Hopefully J.K. Rowling will not only inspire more young people to read, but maybe encourage a few of them to pen tales of their own. Let's hope so. Otherwise the future of entertainment will be nothing more than reality show retreads and the latest dunce posting on You Tube.

Thanks for introducing a new generation of readers to big books, Harry. Sorry I crap on you in the next piece. I truly enjoy your wizarding world!

HARRY POTTER AND THE
PRETENTIOUS BOOK REVIEWER

July 2015

I made a social blunder recently when I disparaged *Harry Potter* during a family vacation.

I started reading the *Harry Potter* series this summer, along with my wife and our 11-year-old daughter. There are lots of *Harry Potter* fans in our extended family. I have several nieces and nephews who grew up with author J.K. Rowling's books and movies. My niece recently visited The Wizarding World of Harry Potter in Florida to celebrate her graduation...from college!

These were hardcore fans. I should have known better when they asked what I thought of the first book in the series, *Harry Potter and the Sorcerer's Stone.*

"It's kind of childish," I said. "Heavy-handed. Does the bad kid at school need to be named Draco Malfoy, and his thug friends Crabbe and Goyle? Is Goyle's first name Gar? I understand these characters are snakes in the grass, but do they need to live in Slytherin House, too?"

Everyone looked at me slack-jawed, like I'd blasted a wet shart right there in front of the group. Really, Uncle Rob? Are you *that* guy, the one who finds fault with things that everybody else likes?

Well, yeah, I am that guy. I'm a book reviewer, a "literary critic." (*bobsbookblog.com*). I'm supposed to kick the tires and pick at the seams of novels and short stories, check the quality of their build, see how they function, and let people know if they deliver the literary goods.

I tried to clarify my *Harry Potter* stance with my wife later on.

"There's a simple beauty to J.K. Rowling's work, the way some of the best songs are built around three chords. It's catchy, gets your heart pumping, and sweeps you away. That's the magic of *Harry Potter*. It's like a great pop song you can't stop humming," I explained.

"But I don't appreciate Rowling's running gag with the character names. It took me out of the story," I said. "There's no reason to name your characters Billy Badguy, Sally Sidekick, or Lucy Loveinterest."

"What if you had a character named Bob Buzzkill?" my wife asked. "Or Peter Pretentious. Or Biggie Blackcloud. He'd be a mopey Native American who makes it rain on everybody's parade."

"Funny, but that's not me," I said. "I'm a journalist! I dissect the subject to get to the truth! I'd be Chris Critic! Geraldo Reviewer!"

"Jerky McJealous," my wife countered. "Write your own bestselling young adult series if you don't like *Harry Potter*."

Clearly this is not an argument I'm meant to win. Nor do I want to.

Because I like *Harry Potter*! I'm new to Rowling's Wizarding World, but already I can see it's filled with memorable adventures and unforgettable characters. I don't know if it's a modern literary classic, but it's certainly well crafted and delightfully designed. Harry Potter is built with love and built to last.

So what if I have quibbles with Rowling's character names? It's certainly not the first thing I should mention when people ask how I like the Harry Potter series. But I have poor social skills, and I'm...I'm...

Igor Ignorant. Arnie Awkward. Jack Ass. Dullard Scott.

Donald Dummy. Yushur Head. Hugh Jassel. Robert Galbraith?

SOLVING THE HARRY POTTER WHODUNNIT

July 2013

Question: Who killed debut novelist Robert Galbraith? Where did the murder take place, and what weapon was used?

Answer: The Lawyer's Wife's Friend did it, in the Public Eye, with her Twitter Account.

Harry Potter author J. K. Rowling published a detective novel called *The Cuckoo's Calling* under the pen name Robert Galbraith earlier this year. The book had a small distribution, decent reviews, and meager sales.

Two weeks ago, *The Sunday Times* of London ran a story that revealed Robert Galbraith was J.K. Rowling's *nom de plume*. Apparently a friend of the wife of a lawyer at Rowling's law firm spilled the beans on her Twitter account. (She later deleted the tweets, but the cat was out of the bag.)

Imagine creating something—a building, a painting, a song, a software application, a reputation—that grows so big and popular, you no longer own or control it. The creation overshadows—and stifles—the creator. You can't get away. It follows you everywhere, haunting you like Frankenstein's monster.

This is a common problem among artists, especially those who score a "breakout hit" early in their career. Radiohead hit big with the single "Creep" in 1992. But the band struggled with mega-stardom, and wrote about it in the follow-up single, "My Iron Lung" (1994). It's a great metaphor; an iron lung both sustains and imprisons you, gives you life, but holds you captive.

I don't know if J.K. Rowling was experiencing Frankenstein Syndrome or Iron Lung-itis when she decided to publish a detective novel under the Galbraith name. Writers use pseudonyms for a variety of reasons. Sometimes they want to distance themselves from their more well-known works, or works in other genres. Sometimes they're looking to redefine themselves as authors. Sometimes it's a marketing strategy. Sometimes they're looking for another revenue stream. Sometimes they want to know if their work is still valid without the aid of a bankable name.

It's easy to imagine Rowling trapped in the iron lung of *Harry Potter*. The franchise is huge, beyond anything Rowling can personally control. While it will sustain Rowling (probably several generations of Rowlings) and afford her financial freedom, it's difficult to see J.K. Rowling as anything other than the creator of the *Harry Potter* series. It probably always will be.

It must be frustrating for Rowling. She's done with adolescent fantasy—she wants to sink her teeth into a juicy mystery! It's hard for any commercially successful artist to branch out, stay original, and avoid the "sophomore curse." I'm sure Psy has penned a soulful love ballad as a follow-up to "Gangnam Style," but we're never going to hear it. People like the tried and true—be creative, but don't

77

change lanes or color outside the box.

Once upon a time, writers used pseudonyms to attract a bigger audience. Female authors like Mary Ann Evans (George Eliot), Amandine Lucie Aurore Dupin (George Sand), and Alice Sheldon (James Tiptree, Jr.) used male pen names to break into the male-dominated world of publishing.

But Rowling seems to seek a *smaller* audience, or, at the very least, a different type of reader than the legions of *Harry Potter* fans.

Was Rowling's decision to write under a pen name an artistic choice, or a clever marketing ploy? We may never know. Rowling claims she was "unmasked" against her will, but her protests sound hollow, like "celebrities" who act shocked and indignant when a professionally shot, edited, and packaged sex tape "mysteriously surfaces."

Either way, the days of using a pen name seem numbered. The modern media—powered by an amateur army of social-media savvy, camera-phone packin' celebrity gawkers— makes it impossible to keep anything a secret for long.

RIP, Mr. Galbraith. We hardly knew ye.

Publishing is a harsh mistress, but the way it caresses the ego is irresistible, especially if you're a starry-eyed, teenage poet…

VANITY, THY NAME IS PUBLISHING

November 2011

Like most writers, my early work stunk (and, some would say, hasn't much improved). But, like many fledging writers who made their bones in the '80s/'90s, I submitted my crappy, sappy work to places like Vantage Press and The National Library of Poetry.

Unlike most publishers, these guys didn't reject my work. They'd happily include me in their next poetry anthology...as long as I bought a copy of the book for $40.

Welcome to the vanity press, where you essentially pay somebody to publish your work. It was, and pretty much always should be, the lowest rung of the publishing ladder.

When I started out, self-publishing was for losers. Yes, there are great writers who have successfully self-published— *Ulysses* by James Joyce, *A Time To Kill* by John Grisham, and much of Edgar Allan Poe's work. But self-publishing was mainly for weak writers who weren't good enough to get their work approved by a real editor at a real publishing house.

The goal was to land a deal with one of the "Big 6" publishing houses: Hachette Book Group, MacMillan Publishing, HarperCollins, Penguin Group, Random House, or Simon & Schuster. They could write you a big advance check, book you appearances on Jay Leno and Howard Stern, and promote your book with giant kiosks in bookstores around the globe.

But the odds of that happening are the same as winning the lottery. Landing a book deal is incredibly difficult, and even when you do, most authors find themselves stuck in the mid-list, where authors get little or no advance and even less marketing support. Promoting a book is often a do-it-yourself effort. So why not publish the thing yourself, and see if you can sell enough copies to cover the printing costs?

Distribution used to be the main stumbling block for self-published authors. Local stores might stock your book, but how do you get your work into the hands of a wider audience?

Technology has changed the way books are printed, distributed, and even read. Most books are bought online, which makes it easier for self-published authors to get the same distribution as authors published by the Big Six. The rise of ebooks/ereaders and print-on-demand technology leveled the playing field even further.

Today, self-publishing doesn't quite have the stink it used to. In fact, some authors have found it a lucrative alternative to traditional publishing deals. *The Shack*, a Christian novel by William P. Young, was self-published in 2007, and went on to sell a million copies by June 2008. Amanda Hocking began self-publishing her paranormal romance novels as e-books in April 2010. By March 2011 she'd sold over a million copies, and earned well over two million dollars. She recently signed another two million dollar deal with St. Martin's Press.

The times they are a-changin', and now the real vanity seems to be waiting around for one of the Big Six to discover your work and toss fame and fortune into your lap. It's vanity to need the approval of a New York editor and Random House's logo on the spine of your book.

Let's face it, all writers (at least those who submit their work for public consumption) are vain to a certain degree. We all want to wow everyone with our smooth style, clever vocabulary, and powerful stories.

Today it's easy to get your book(s) out in the marketplace. Why wait for an editor/publisher to decide if your stuff is something people will like? Let the buying public decide.

I've dipped my toe into the waters of self-publishing, too. You can find my stuff online. But this isn't a plug for my books (well, kinda…). It's about the changing landscape of publishing. Despite my DIY approach, I'd still like to see my writing endorsed by a big publishing house. (If any Random House editors are reading, no offense!) As much as I downplayed it in the paragraphs above, getting your work accepted by a "real editor" is precious indeed. Even a kindly worded rejection letter can give a writer the motivation to keep writing, especially in these early days, when your work stinks and sales are nil.

I still have the Honorable Mention pin I received from the National Library of Poetry back in 1987. My poem didn't win a money prize in the poetry contest, but it did make a short list of honorable mentions. They don't give those pins out to just anybody, you know. You have to demonstrate real writing skill.

Rob Errera

And have $40 to buy the book.

I still have that crappy $40 poetry book. It's called Many Voices,
Many Lands *and it contains my first "professionally" published piece.
I still have the Honorable Mention pin, too. It's stuck to the front of
my bass guitar…my poetic license!*

THE MAGAZINE IS DEAD! LONG LIVE THE MAGAZINE!

April 2014

I love magazines. For years, I earned a living running a magazine, and I still write for a bunch of titles. I enjoy the articles, interviews, and photography magazines deliver.

But I haven't bought a magazine at a newsstand in years, and you probably haven't either. Print magazines are dinosaurs in the age of the Internet, and you can hear the great beasts screaming from the tar pits.

The latest to go under is *The Ladies Home Journal*, which has published for an astonishing 131 years! A web site will continue, but the magazine will be reformatted as a quarterly special interest publication. (That means four times a year you'll see something like "Ladies Home Journal presents Favorite Holiday Recipes," or "LHJ's Spring Fashion Fling," on newsstands.) All of the magazine's editorial staff was laid off last month.

The *Ladies Home Journal* began publishing in 1883, and was the first American magazine to reach one million subscribers back in 1903. For decades, *LHJ* had the highest circulation of any magazine in America. *LHJ* was one of publishing's original "Seven Sisters"—magazines aimed at married female homemakers and stay-at-home moms. The other sisters include *Better Homes and Gardens, Good Housekeeping, Family Circle, Redbook, Woman's Day*, and *McCall's* (defunct since 2002).

The Seven Sisters had divergent beginnings. *Family Circle* began as a circular for Piggly Wiggly grocery store, and *Woman's Day* as an A&P flyer. *McCall's* and *Redbook* were known for longer works of fiction and nonfiction. *Better Homes and Gardens* tried to blend women's interest with a home design journal.

The Ladies Home Journal began as a one-page supplement called *Women at Home* in a magazine called *Tribune and Farmer* published by Cyrus H.K. Curtis. Curtis' wife, Louisa Knapp Curtis, edited *Women at Home*, which was so popular, it was launched as its own magazine in 1884, called *The Ladies Home Journal and Practical Housekeeper*. The last three words were dropped from the title two years later. Since 1946, *The Ladies Home Journal* has used the apt slogan, "Never underestimate the power of a woman". Now *LHJ* is nothing but another faded American brand, a URL leading to a web portal.

It's sad watching magazines die off. The slick pages and glossy covers we grew up with will be extinct by the next generation. Gone are phone book-sized editions of *PC Magazine* (1982-2009), the cool blend of art, business, and design inside *I.D. Magazine* (1954-2010), and the crinkly pages and concise summaries of *Newsweek* (1933-2012).

Where did magazines go? Well, there's an app for that. *U.S. News & World Report* ceased print publication in 2010, but lives on in the digital realm. *Radar* published from 2003-2008 before establishing its online presence. Like backwards butterflies, the fluttering pages of periodicals are undergoing a metamorphosis, becoming click-and-zoom mobile websites, digital editions on virtual newsstands, or downloadable apps for smartphones and tablets.

The Magazine is dead!

Long live The Magazine!

Books are dead, too. Long live books!

TOSS OUT THE BOOKSHELF, NOT THE BOOKS

October 2011

Books are beautiful.

Their construction is so basic—paper, ink, glue, and cardboard. But each is a doorway into another time and space, alternate dimensions both real and imagined.

It doesn't matter if you're reading true crime, historical fiction, or a cookbook; all are woven from the fabric of the human condition. Books are a reflection of us, who we are, where we've come from, and where we might be headed. Books offer a double whammy of knowledge and enlightenment coupled with escapism and fun, simultaneously invigorating and relaxing.

Books have been my friends and teachers since childhood. I loved cracking open a new book when I was a kid (still do). The smell and feel of crisp pages beneath my fingers felt like opening a treasure chest. I borrowed from the library often, and learned to appreciate the beauty of well-thumbed books, too. The ghosts of old dog-ears, the depth of the creases in the spine, and the occasional handwritten note in the margin told the story of all the people who had touched—and been touched by—this book. Who else feasted upon this tome, and how did their mind digest its contents?

Once upon a time, before the modern printing press (itself a dinosaur facing extinction), books were rare, precious commodities. They still are, and always will be. Because books are the *ideas* and the *words* used to express those ideas, not the ink and paper they're delivered on. Books are created in the heart and mind of the author, and live in the hearts and minds of readers. The bound stack of pages with writing on them is merely a transfer method. There are other ways to read a book now.

Digital books, ebooks, are the new "dime paperbacks," cheap and easy to distribute. Traditional publishing houses need to either embrace this new technology or face extinction. You don't have to look any further than the nearest abandoned Borders to see the future of print publishing.

Publishers should sell print editions that come with free/discounted links to ebook and audiobook formats. Print-on-demand technology allows authors to sell reasonably priced print editions—even signed editions—to fans who want to put something on their bookshelves. These new technologies are changing—in fact, have changed—the face of the publishing industry.

In the 1990s, the rise of digital music formats—and sites like Napster—caught the record companies off-guard. Sony, BMI, and the other biggies were reluctant to say goodbye to the $18 CD, but eventually settled on a $9.99 iTunes download. Similarly, book publishers need to bid farewell to the $30 hardcover, and embrace a lower priced ebook format.

History may repeat in another way. Musical artists learned a decade ago they really didn't need the support of giant record companies to connect with fans. They could do it themselves with You Tube, Facebook, and Twitter (Justin Bieber, anyone?). Authors may discover the same thing, finding an audience for their work without needing the support and approval of a handful of big New York publishers.

I learned to separate a book from its content when I became a book buyer. I'd read paperbacks because they were inexpensive, and easy to transport. It wasn't a tragedy if I left one on the bus, or dropped it in the bathtub. If I read something I really enjoyed, I'd seek it out in hardcover, or— back when I could afford it (i.e., pre-kids)—in a signed, limited edition. Over the years I amassed a sizeable collection.

But I donated most of my books to the local library last year when we relocated/remodeled. I figured I'll replace my favorite books with digital editions over time, much like I have done with my music collection.

But I miss my books, the fading covers and yellowing pages. My wife tells me to stop whining, there's less on the shelves to gather dust, and I suppose she's right. (Isn't she always?) I'd already read all the books I donated, consumed their contents, and if I wanted a refresher, I could find what I needed on the Internet.

Still, I miss my books…

Newspapers…also dead! Long live newspapers!

NEWSPAPER LOVERS! NEVER FEAR! AMAZON CEO JEFF BEZOS IS HERE!

September 2013

Look! Up in the sky! It's a bird! It's a plane!

It's Amazon CEO Jeff Bezos, swooping in like Superman to save the newspaper industry!

Last month Bezos bought *The Washington Post* from the Graham family, which has owned the veritable newspaper for four generations. Bezos paid $250 million in cash for the newspaper, and will become its sole owner when the sale is complete this fall.

Critics called the sale the end of *The Post's* commitment to journalistic integrity. *The Washington Post* has a long tradition of distinguished news reporting, including breaking the story of the Watergate cover-up in the early 1970s.

But Jeff Bezos didn't just buy *The Washington Post*. He saved it from certain destruction. Newspapers have been in a downward spiral ever since the birth of the Internet. Readership and print advertising budgets are shrinking. Newspapers are either folding up shop, or getting folded into media conglomerates.

"*The Post* could have survived under the company's ownership, and been profitable for the foreseeable future. But we wanted to do more than survive," *The Post* quoted Chairman and CEO Donald E. Graham as saying. "I'm not saying this guarantees success, but it gives us a much greater chance of success."

There's no reason to believe *The Post* will waiver in its journalistic commitment because Bezos is at the helm. If anything, it's likely to improve.

Bezos creates quality products and services that change the way we live. The same way Steve Jobs and Apple changed the way we listened to music and used our phones and personal computers, Jeff Bezos changed the way we shop with Amazon. The Kindle ereader changed the way we read books. We can assume Bezos will ultimately use his purchase of *The Washington Post* to change the way people read newspapers, too.

According to columnist Michael Hendrix: "Journalism is undergoing a structural shift. Old forms of journalism are fading away. Other industries are rising to perform similar functions of spreading information and shining light into dark places."

What is the role of the newspaper in the digital age? How can it survive?

"In my experience, the way invention, innovation, and change happen are through team effort. There's no lone genius who figures it all out, and sends down the magic formula," Bezos said in a recent interview in *The Post*. "You study, you debate, you brainstorm, and the answers start to emerge."

Bezos admits there are no "quick fixes" for the newspaper's problems.

"It takes time. Nothing happens quickly in this mode. You develop theories and hypotheses, but you don't know if readers will respond. You do as many experiments as rapidly as possible. 'Quickly' in my mind would be years."

I have no doubt Bezos will find a way to revitalize *The Post*, along with the rest of the newspaper industry. Whether it's a new device, a new platform, or a new business model, Bezos has the vision, the resources, and the financial means to make it so.

Save us, Mr. Bezos! And make drones deliver on Sundays. I want Amazon packages raining from the sky 24-7!

WRITERS ON STRIKE, ENTERTAINMENT ON HOLD

January 2008

I'm not a big fan of labor unions. For starters, they don't recognize individual achievement. Example: Joe and Pete are both members of the Meat Packers union. Joe works twice as hard as Pete but, at the end of the year, both will be awarded the same 3.5% pay raise their union leader negotiated for them. Where is Joe's incentive to work harder next year? Where's Pete's punishment for slacking off?

Second, labor strikes always smack of extortion. Workers get hired to do a certain job. But unionized workers sometimes decide they're not going to do their jobs unless they get something more—more benefits, more safety measures, more money. It doesn't matter to the striking workers if their work stoppage disrupts the lives of others—like when the New York City transit workers went on strike in 2005. In fact, these disruptions demonstrate just how valuable workers are, and how management should give in to their demands.

People have every right to ask for a pay raise or better working conditions. If their boss doesn't give in, they have every right to leave. And if they stop working, their boss has every right to fire them.

That being said, I stand in solidarity with the striking Writers Guild of America. No, I'm not a member of the guild. But I'm a guy who makes a living toying with language and tinkering with written words, so I feel a kinship with the Guild.

The Writers Guild is squaring off against the Alliance of Motion Picture and Television Producers (AMPTP). One of the main issues is disagreement over "new media"—the distribution of TV shows and movies over the Internet and through video-on-demand outlets. The WGA has proposed that writers receive 2.5% of distributor's gross for new-media sales and distribution. The AMPTP says that new media is an "unproven medium" and refuses to pay writers anything.

The problem is that the AMPTP used the "unproven medium" argument 20 years ago when VHS tapes were "new media." They used it again in 1996 when DVDs began to replace VHS tapes in the home video market. In fact, Hollywood studios readily admit that DVD sales have become their biggest moneymakers. Between January and March of 2004, consumers spent $1.8 billion at the box office and $4.8 billion on DVD sales. Yet they continue to offer writers the same measly residual percentage they did in 1988 when the home video market was in its infancy.

Writers feel Hollywood producers have shortchanged them for years. Clearly, Internet distribution and video-on-demand will become the primary way people watch TV shows and movies in the not-so-distant future. The writers don't want the same raw deal they got when the home video market was emerging 20 years ago. Who can blame them? Hollywood producers may not have found a way to make money yet off downloaded movies and television shows, but they will. When they do, they should give the writers who helped create such programs their rightful slice of the pie.

In the meantime, prepare to hunker down on your entertainment haunches (the 1988 writer's strike lasted nearly 22 weeks; this current strike is 10 weeks old and shows no sign of resolution) and amuse yourself with reruns, a slew of new reality and game shows, and bearded late-night hosts ad-libbing monologues. My advice: go out and buy a couple of good books; there are plenty of writers on the bookstore shelves who could use your support, too.

The 2007-2008 writer's strike lasted 14 weeks and cost $1.5 million in lost production costs. Writers, united, are a powerful group! Smart, too. Subscription services and video streaming has proved worthy "new media." The writers behind The Twilight Zone *could even predict the future!*

PROZAC NATION GETS ITS SMILE ON

July 2007

"Don't worry, dear. You're just nervous. What you need is a glass of Instant Smile!"

It's one of my favorite lines from one of my favorite shows: *The Twilight Zone* episode titled, "Number 12 Looks Just Like You," adapted from a story by Charles Beaumont. A young girl is urged by her mother (and doctor) to accept a cloning procedure that will leave her looking (and thinking) like all the rest of her friends and family. Mom wants her daughter to pick a tall buxom model ("Number 12"), but the daughter is worried about losing her individuality. Her mom, and doctor, recommend a glass of Instant Smile, a cure-all beverage that seems to mellow everyone out and leave them blissfully, if ignorantly, happy.

America is close to making the Instant Smile experience a reality. A recent report by the U.S. Centers for Disease Control revealed that antidepressant drugs are now the most commonly prescribed drugs in America. Doctors write more scripts for Paxil, Prozac, Lexapro, etc. than they do for meds to treat high blood pressure, high cholesterol, asthma, or headaches.

This news isn't surprising. The boom of direct-to-consumer prescription drug advertising ("Ask your doctor about…") has caused the use of antidepressants to more than triple in the last 15 years. People who ask their doctor for an antidepressant usually get one.

In one way this is a good sign. Depression is a major public health issue, and people are finally getting the treatment they need. I've seen antidepressant drugs help people turn their lives around. Antidepressant drugs can save lives.

But you have to question the number of "clinically depressed" people popping pills in this country. Dr. Ronald Dworkin tells a story in his book, *Artificial Unhappiness: The Dark Side of the New Happy Class,* about a woman who was unhappy with her husband's handling of the family finances. She wanted to take over the job, but didn't want to insult her husband. Her doctor suggested she try an antidepressant to make herself feel better.

"Doctors are now medicating unhappiness," said Dworkin. "Too many people take drugs when they really need to be making changes in their lives."

You don't have to be all Scientologist / Tom Cruise-kooky to see there's a drug abuse problem in this country that is being propagated by the medical community and their prescription pads. One of the reasons for the sharp rise in prescription drug use is that doctors—much to the profitable pleasure of pharmaceutical manufacturers—are combining different drugs together, tailoring them to suit the needs of individual patients. It's not uncommon for antidepressant users to be on two, three, or more different types of medication as they search for the "cocktail" that works best for them. Everybody's cup of Instant Smile has its own, unique flavor.

But you're supposed to feel things. Sadness and pain are part of life, and working through these emotions is part of what it means to be alive, to be human. Drugs shouldn't be a band-aid for deeper psychological problems, and they shouldn't be used as a crutch to get through the trials of daily living.

There are many times when I long for a tall, cool glass of Instant Smile. I've tried creating my own Instant Smile cocktail on occasion using alcohol, chocolate, tobacco, brick-oven pizzas, and other secret ingredients, but results are mixed. Nothing quite recreates the sudden forgetful nirvana pictured on *The Twilight Zone*, though the drone-like populace and tyrannical government are starting to look familiar.

I'll keep trying.

Turn on! Tune in! Drop out! That's the signpost up ahead—your next stop, Rock 'n' Roll!

Raised On
Rock 'n' Roll

MAGICAL JOURNEY INTO MYSTERY TOUR

January 2019

I love rock 'n' roll! Put another dime in the jukebox, baby!

As puberty gave way to young adulthood, rock music supplanted comic books as my main source of education and entertainment.

Each album in Brother Mike's record collection was like a novel, each song an exciting new chapter. I didn't like it all, but I found gems that appealed to my young ears. Mott The Hoople, Mick Ronson, and the scary Winter brothers, Edgar and Johnny, who looked like comic-book creatures. My favorite album was all black except for a rainbow prism in the center of the cover, and featured alarm clocks, snippets of whispered conversations, and sad, beautiful songs. I brought my brother's copy of *Dark Side Of The Moon* to school for second grade show-and-tell. My teacher looked at the album and laughed. She didn't play it for the class. I couldn't understand why.

Brother Mike's record collection was a doorway, a magic carpet that transported me to new worlds. Music was a transitive experience even more immersive and engaging than comic books. Whatever the question, music had the answer.

MODERN CONCERTS ARE BIG ON SPECTACLE

October 2014

Once upon a time, I loved going to rock concerts.

It didn't matter what the act was. Tickets were cheap in the 1980s: $15-$20; maybe $27.50 for fancy seats.

One week in the mid-'80s I saw REO Speedwagon on a Monday night, and KISS that Thursday. I was at an Ozzy Osbourne/Metallica show where the crowd ripped apart the seats and tossed seat cushions around the arena until a swirling cloud of cushions hovered above the arena floor. I thought there was a fire when Rage Against the Machine played the Lollapalooza Festival in 1993, but it wasn't smoke; it was the mosh pit kicking up a funnel of dry dust in front of the stage. A decade earlier Brian Johnson walked down our aisle with Angus Young on his shoulders during an AC/DC concert at the Brendon Byrne area. It really impressed my girlfriend at the time.

Back in the day, the Brendan Byrne Arena and Giants Stadium were the main concert venues for big touring acts in North Jersey. Both venues are still around, but they've become the Izod Center and Metlife Stadium, respectively.

I hadn't been to a big rock concert in over a decade, but I was happy to take my 10-year-old daughter and her friend to see One Direction at Metlife Stadium. Live music is awesome and I was eager to indoctrinate my daughter into the rock concert experience.

Making our way into Metlife Stadium, I noticed a trend; it seemed most parents were waiting in the parking lot, tailgating, while their kids went into the concert. Not me. I was there for the music, man! Plus, my daughter's only 10. I wasn't going to send her and her friend into Metlife Stadium by themselves.

One Direction played a fine set, though the emphasis was more on explosions, fireworks, streamers, and balloons rather than music. During the power ballad, everybody held up the flashlight app on their cell phones and waved them back and forth. I wondered what happened to all the cigarette lighters, but then I realized nobody smokes anymore and lighters are dangerous.

The One Direction concert came off a bit impersonal, but I can't blame the band. They're just following a trend that began years ago, back when I was still a regular concertgoer.

Giant video screens have been around at rock concerts since the early '80s, and while they are supposed to make big stadium shows feel cozy, instead they reduce live performance to a TV show. Why watch the little man with the guitar from 200 yards away when you can watch the video screen and get a close-up? Why even *go* to a live concert at all when you can watch the same video footage from the comfort of your home?

Before the use of big video screens, bands used stage effects to enhance the music rather than distract from it. From the mid-'60s and into the '70s, rock bands had liquid light shows or psychedelic light shows projected behind them while they played. The swirling, colorful amoeba shapes were eventually replaced by elaborate lighting rigs that synched with the dynamics of the music. The Genesis light show was a selling point for the band's live performances well into the 1980s.

But as technology advanced, an intimacy was lost in the concert-going experience. Giant video screens simultaneously brought audiences closer to the performers and reduced them to characters on TV. I saw several fans recording the concert with their camera phones, but instead of focusing on the members of the band, they were recording the images on the video screens. Why?

One thing that hasn't changed about modern concerts is the energy created when fans gather together to celebrate the music they enjoy. This is the core essence of the concert experience, the same blueprint as religious gatherings. I enjoyed many Grateful Dead concerts over the years, and the atmosphere was very close to a church mass. There was the same sense of reverence, respect, ritual, and release.

And hopefully that will never change. Long live rock 'n' roll!

And glory be to corporate sponsors!

Rob Errera

ROCK 'N' ROLL MONSTER SLAIN BY ITS CREATORS

October 2005

Rock 'n' roll music is a big, pulsating monster, but, like Frankenstein's creature, it is in danger of being destroyed by the very men who helped create it.

The killers are The Rolling Stones, The Who, Paul McCartney, and reunited supergroup Cream. Their weapon is greed. All of these aging rock 'n' roll acts have two things in common: their tours are funded by huge corporate sponsors, and they're charging hundreds of dollars for concert tickets.

Isn't having a big financial sponsor like Fidelity Investments or American Express supposed to help keep ticket prices *down*? Evidently it's just the opposite. Fidelity Investments and American Express are only interested in reaching people

106

who can afford $400 concert tickets. People with that kind of disposable income would be far more likely to use their financial services than the hip-hop crowd at a 50 Cent show or the teeny-boppers flocking to see Britney Spears. The only people who can afford Gold Circle seats are balding, bloated bean-counters and spoiled rich kids, both of whom will be checking their Rolexes by the end of the fifth song, wondering if they should cut out early to beat the traffic and get back home to their Direct TV and TiVos. Anybody who buys "cheap seats" (only $100 –$175) will end up watching most of the show on oversized video monitors. Seems like a hefty price tag to sit in a crowded stadium and watch TV.

Rock 'n' roll, at its core, is the music of rebellion. But the corporate message being sent by The Rolling Stones and Paul McCartney tours is one of compliance. It's not about taking risks, it's about acting responsibly. This isn't about setting your guitar on fire and choking on your own vomit; it's about sound fiscal planning and creating a diversified portfolio. Check out what Ameriquest has to say about its sponsorship of the Rolling Stones.

"The Rolling Stones offer Ameriquest a broad platform to strategically communicate our brand, our services and our positioning as, 'Proud Sponsor of the American Dream,'" said Brian Woods, Ameriquest's Chief Marketing Officer. "In today's saturated marketplace, the Rolling Stones break through the clutter to reach fans in a way that few iconic brands can."

Rock on, Brian! Way to "strategically communicate your brand," dude! The Stones are one of our favorite "iconic brands"!

Therein lies the problem; rock bands (in fact, practically *all* entertainment entities) are now viewed as "iconic brands" which can be used to sell everything from banks, to mortgage companies, to SUVs. The fans who used to pack their concerts in the early days have grown up to become the captains of industry that now support their tours, the same pinheads who think slapping a Who song into their commercial will make me want to buy their allergy medicine.

The soul of these classic rock tunes, their message and meaning, is leached of all its original power, auctioned off to the highest bidder like pork belly futures. As they approach retirement age, the pioneers of rock music have not grown old gracefully; they've grown fat and greedy. As a result, The Great Beast Rock 'n' Roll lies slumped over and dying, the lifeblood that once coursed so mightily through its veins now thin, sickly, and diseased.

The Great Beast Rock 'n' Roll wants to sell you a Coke and a smile.

FOR SALE: YOUR MOST INTIMATE MUSICAL MEMORIES

December 2007

When it was announced recently that Led Zeppelin, after being asked for more than 20 years, was finally permitting one of their songs to be used in a Cadillac commercial, it wasn't much of a news story. After all, the music of The Beatles, Bob Dylan, The Who, and The Rolling Stones has been used to sell everything—from computers, to cars, to cans of beer—for years.

Today, you'd be hard pressed to find a recording artist who *doesn't* auction their latest hit off to the highest bidder. In the '60s and '70s, musicians who licensed their songs for commercial use were labeled sell-outs and were often ridiculed by their fans. Today, recording artists can't sell out fast enough and nobody seems to mind. You'd expect Britney Spears to shill for Pepsi and the Backstreet Boys to yodel for Chili's babyback ribs; these artists were formed by corporate suits, so it's completely natural for them to sing about topics as weighty as carbonated soft drinks and fast food.

Check the pop charts today—within eight weeks these songs will be backing television commercials. In some cases this works to the artist's advantage. Barenaked Ladies (who actually *have* songwriting talent) not only sold the rights to their hit single "One Week" to Mitsubishi, but their sing-along anthem, "If I Had a Million Dollars," is all over radio and TV as part of the New York Lottery promotion. As a result, millions more people are exposed to the Ladies music than would have otherwise been possible. Still, how embarrassing is it when someone recognizes them and points, "Hey, it's those guys who wrote the Lotto commercial!"? I guess big royalty checks help ease the shame.

The most heinous example of this is the use of Pink's "I'm Coming Out" in Bally's Health Club commercials. The first time I heard Pink's song I thought it was a goof.

"They must have gotten some unauthorized tapes of Britney Spears or Christina Aguilera singing off key," I said, turning up the radio. "Listen, she's singing the whole song flat. Oh, it's awful…ha, ha, ha!"

But the joke was on me when I learned that not only was "I'm Coming Out" a real song, it was a big hit. I can forgive the shallow lyrics and repetitive drum machine beat—this is the pathetic standard for modern pop music. But don't people hear Pink singing off key? I blame the decline of music programs in schools—why else would people embrace a song that's so blatantly bad? But it doesn't matter if a song is bad or not—if it's popular, then advertising execs can use it to promote product.

Nobody writes original commercial jingles anymore, which is sheer laziness on the part of the advertising industry. (Petland Discounts—"for the best care a pet can get"—is the only one that comes to mind.) In fact, most people under the age of 25 probably don't even know what a commercial jingle is. But The Big Mac Song ("two all-beef patties, special sauce, lettuce, cheese, pickles, onions, on a sesame seed bun...") and Burger King's "Have It Your Way" anthem ("Hold the pickle, hold the lettuce, special orders don't upset us...") appear as high art compared to inserting the latest pop hit into a soft drink commercial. Advertising execs think it's a safe bet to use familiar songs to sell their products rather than commissioning an unproven jingle. But what they're doing is stealing the emotional content of popular music and using it to sell SUVs and new sneakers. They're mining our memories and using the emotional attachments to sell us poorly made, over-priced junk. It makes me despise big companies and the products they sell all the more.

I used to despise the artists who sold out, but I don't blame Barenaked Ladies or Pink. Management companies and record labels ripped off artists for decades. Now artists have the opportunity to make fast cash—and lots of it—and reach millions of people. (If I were Pink, I'd grab every dollar I could before someone realized I couldn't sing.)

I blame the advertising firms who think the American people are too stupid and too shallow to relate to anything but a melody we've heard a million times before. All the great poets have gone off and joined the world of advertising, and now the great (and many not-so-great) musicians have followed suit. Before long, the works of Pablo Picasso will be used to sell Gap sweaters and Robert Mapplethorpe's photos will be used to plug The Leather Warehouse. I guess that's the pitfall of living in a capitalist society; everything has a pricetag, and if you can't market it to the masses, it's

111

worthless.

Such is the sorry state of "art" in America.

Maybe Andres Serrano's Piss Christ *to sell Mike's Hard Lemonade? Anyone? Oh...sorry, Pink. I guess you've got more talent and staying power than I originally thought. You're a rock star! You've got your rock moves!*

SELLING THE ROCK STAR EXPERIENCE

November 2007

Once upon a time I was a rock star.

Well, not really, but I played bass in a band. We recorded a few CDs, played a bunch of local bars, and had a good following. Some nights—when the band was on, and the crowd was bouncing to the beat, and the whole room was shaking—I *felt* like a rock star. It was a good feeling. No, it was a *great* feeling.

But, despite these experiences, I've never considered myself a "real" musician. A real musician reads and writes music. A real musician sits down at a piano with sheet music they've never seen before and plays the tune. Real musicians understand the theory behind those groups of notes on the musical staff. I'm a guy who wanted to be a rock star, so I took a few lessons, practiced a lot, and got good enough to get a little taste of the real thing. It was a lot of work, a lot of play; either way it was a lot of time invested.

113

But now the Rock Star Experience can be had by anyone, with minimal effort. You can even become a Real Life Rock Star and have no musical ability whatsoever. Consider the following examples:

1. *Guitar Hero III by Activision.* I'm not a video game buff; I lost interest after *Space Invaders* and *Pac Man.* But this is the hottest video game on the market, the "big gift" this holiday season. It comes with a plastic guitar controller and you press buttons on a fretboard based on on-screen prompts. Like all video games, it requires finger dexterity and good eye/hand coordination. The irony of *Guitar Hero* is that if you spent the same time practicing on an *actual guitar* as you did mastering this game, you could *actually play guitar.* Put down the controller and pick up a guitar!

2. *Jam Sessions for Nintendo DS.* This is another hand-held computer game, but there are no high scores, mind-blowing graphics, etc. Instead, this piece of software allows you to strum your Nintendo DS game system like an air guitar and make music come out. Now anyone can lead a campfire sing-a-long as long as they have their Nintendo DS. The only skill you need beyond the ability to push a button is the ability to move your arm back and forth in a strumming motion. Hey, if playing guitar is this easy, why would anyone waste time learning to play a real guitar ever again?

3. *Fatboy Slim Live At Brighton Beach.* I caught this 2002 concert film on one of the pay channels by some fluke and was mystified. It was a rock concert, but there was no band. There was music, but no musicians. Fatboy Slim is not an obese hip-hop thug; he's a skinny white Englishman, balding and dweeby. His talent is mixing bits of other songs and sound bites together over a droning electronic drum beat. He's making music, but he's not a musician. I'm not saying some of Fatboy Slim's compositions aren't catchy or enjoyable. But it's surreal watching a crowd of 100,000 people dance around while on stage one guy flips through a

stack of CDs, fiddles with buttons and knobs, and smiles goofily for the camera. It's sad. Have our expectations for entertainment sunk so low? At least other non-musical musical acts like Britney Spears can dance (well, she used too).

My Dad had a corny comeback if anyone asked if he played a musical instrument. "The only thing I can play is the radio," he'd say. Hey Dad, joke's on you—evidently that qualifies now.

Packaging the Rock Star Experience for mass consumption began with karaoke, which allows anyone to sing lead vocals on their favorite song. Now pre-packaged rock stardom has expanded to include guitar playing. Before long you will be able to tap out drum beats with your fingers and sound like John Bonham or Ringo Starr, or run your hands up and down a table top and sound like Billy Joel playing piano. The software already exists. If the success of Fatboy Slim is any indication, you may actually get to *be* a real-life rock star if you get good enough on your non-musical instrument. Don't worry if you're not a "real musician"—nobody else seems to mind. You can even play the radio.

Rock on!

Music is a shared experience…but you can't process and package it like cheese!

YOU CAN'T GO HOME AGAIN WITH
TAKE ME HOME TONIGHT

March 2011

Note to filmmakers, television producers, and music executives: The 1980s were awful.

Seriously, it was an abominable time for entertainment. With a few notable exceptions, the films, music, and television shows of this era were sub-par. It wasn't a very fun time to "come of age" either, with AIDS paranoia tossing a wet blanket on everyone's sexuality, and Nancy Reagan imploring all to "just say no to drugs."

This decade produced some of the worst music ever released. There are only three musical acts of substance to emerge from the 1980s: Metallica, U2, and REM. Oh, and the 1980s saw the rise of rap as a musical art form. Isn't that evidence enough these were the worst of times?

So why is '80s nostalgia still such a potent marketing tool? Why was *Take Me Home Tonight*—a movie based on a bad

Eddie Money song and featuring bad 1980s music—even made? (I think the producers of *Take Me Home Tonight* may have wondered the same thing. This film was made in 2006-2007 and took four years to find a distributor. Sadly, they found one, and now it's playing in a theater near you.)

I grew up in the 1980s, graduated high school in 1986. I knew even as I was lived in those days of Journey and Loverboy they were bad times. I longed for the music of a decade earlier, when great bands like Led Zeppelin and Pink Floyd roamed the rock 'n' roll landscape. When grunge music emerged in the early 1990s, with its back-to-basics bass/guitar/drums sound, I happily jumped on that bandwagon.

One of the reasons the 1980s were so terrible musically was due to technical advances in instruments and recording equipment. Ever notice how most '80s music has the same annoying keyboard sound? That's a Yamaha DX-7, the first mass-marketed digital synthesizer. It was released in 1983, and was immediately overused by every artist who laid hands on it, from Depeche Mode to Thomas Dolby.

MIDI (Musical Instrument Digital Interface) was established in 1982, and allowed several synthesizers and drum machines to be linked together. Music became "programmable." You could create whole songs, whole albums, full symphonies, without needing a human present!

The problem was music lost its humanity. The machines played flawlessly, kept perfect time, and never tired, but they lacked soul.

The early '90s put the emphasis back on songwriting and performing, but more revolutionary technical advances loomed by the end of the decade. Some of these changes were pretty good. Cheap and powerful home recording equipment coupled with the iTunes platform allowed musicians everywhere to easily get their product out to the masses.

Other changes were not so good. Sampling and remixing made it easier to monkey with old songs rather than write new ones. The producer—whose role was once limited to telling the sound engineer, "turn the guitar down and make the vocal louder"—has replaced the songwriter as top dog in the studio. Software-based programs like AutoTune allow the most tone-deaf warbler to sing on key.

The result of this latest round of technical advancement is a music industry filled with non-musicians. It's enough to make you long for a double shot of The Hooters and REO Speedwagon. Yeah, their songs were awful, but at least they wrote and performed those awful songs themselves, using real instruments.

I'm not immune to nostalgia. Bryan Adams' 1984 hit "Summer of '69" will come on the radio, and it will take me back to a time when I was "young and restless, and needed to unwind."

I guess nothing can last forever, no.

In the case of most things '80s, that's a good thing.

My hatred of '80s nostalgia is surely the result of buried childhood drama. It would explain my disgust of Stranger Things. *It would explain so much. But the decade truly was a backstep musically. The 1990s were better…except for Marilyn Manson. He sucks.*

WHY MARILYN MANSON SUCKS

June 1997

He's the Devil. He's the anti-Christ. He's the most evil man in America.

He's Marilyn Manson.

"Who?" the average over-40 person will ask. "You mean that scary-looking rock star they keep showing on the news?"

Yeah, that guy. Lately, the wicked "Mr. M" has been splattered all over the media. Parental and religious groups can't stand him, and are going to great lengths to have his concerts banned in cities across America. The New Jersey Sports and Exposition Authority recently tried to ban Marilyn Manson from this summer's "Ozzfest" at Giants Stadium. (Ironically, Ozzfest is headlined by Ozzy Osbourne, who was dubbed "Devil" and "anti-Christ" himself during his wilder days in the '70s and '80s.)

Fortunately, reasonable heads prevailed, and the First Amendment won out. Marilyn Manson will perform at

Ozzfest as scheduled. The controversy worked wonders for ticket and album sales.

The man behind Marilyn Manson is Brian Warner, a guy with a very American name, if rather skewed American sensibilities. If you listen to rumors, Marilyn Manson really sounds like a hell-spawned demon. "He encourages rape and murder." "He tosses out bags of drugs to audience members." "He hurls puppies and kittens into the audience and demands they be sent back to the stage dead or he won't perform." (Coincidentally, this same rumor surfaced about Ozzy Osbourne back when I was in high school, uh…a couple of years ago.)

Interviews with Brian Warner show that Marilyn Manson is more myth than menace. The rumors about him are largely exaggerated or outright false. Okay, so he *did* sodomize a bandmate on stage and occasionally befouls the American flag. Welcome to "shock rock" in the '90s. He claims his membership in the Church of Satan is no more sinister than his membership at Blockbuster Video or the local library. Listening to this "ultra-freak" whine about being "misunderstood" is a bit of a laugh. Hey, if you're worried about being misquoted, like, don't get your tongue pierced, dude!

To me, the real mystery of Marilyn Manson is the music. In a word, it's awful. Marilyn Manson can't sing, can't write lyrics, and his tunes are a bland blend of stale drum loops and studio tricks. How anyone who's not completely tone deaf would willingly listen to this noise is beyond me.

As a writer/musician, I'm a staunch supporter of First Amendment freedoms, and I'm pleased Marilyn Manson is protected from right wing attacks. But sadly, he has little talent, and even less to say. The First Amendment protects many great works of controversial art, but Marilyn Manson isn't one of them. I wish there was a message worth protecting here, but there isn't.

Poor, misunderstood Marilyn claims he's trying to stress the "importance of being an individual." Funny, this comment coming from a guy whose persona is wholly comprised of retro rock 'n' roll shtick. Didn't we hear this creepy music coming from Alice Cooper during the 1970s? Didn't Kiss already do the make-up thing? Didn't David Bowie and Iggy Pop originate the pale, gaunt rock star look? Sure they did, and they did it many years ago, and they did it better.

The media hype around Marilyn Manson is just that: media hype. It's a clever marketing ploy dreamed up by record company executives to sell a few more albums. Those young hipsters out there pledging allegiance to Marilyn Manson should wise up—even a cursory glance at rock 'n' roll history exposes MM's shallowness. Those over 40 have no need for alarm—not only is Marilyn Manson not the Devil, he's not even a good imitation.

Marilyn Manson is still around, and he still sucks. So does Kanye West.

KANYE AND A CONGRESSMAN HIGHLIGHT THIS WEEK IN RUDENESS

September 2009

The world was once a more civilized, more respectful, more courteous place. Now, extreme displays of public rudeness are becoming commonplace and an icy aloofness toward your fellow man is the norm.

Joe Wilson, a Republican Congressman from South Carolina, flipped out during President Obama's Congressional address earlier this month. Wilson got red in the face, pointing his finger and shouting, "You lie!" when Obama said current health care reform measures would not provide government-subsidized benefits to illegal immigrants. Both political parties were quick to condemn Wilson's outburst, and Wilson was quick to apologize. He forgot it's rude to heckle the president of the United States.

Rapper, record-producer, fashion-designer, and all-around jerk Kanye West upped the rudeness ante last week during the MTV Video Music Awards when he jumped on stage during Taylor Swift's acceptance speech. Kanye questioned the 19-year-old country singer's victory and extolled the virtues of Beyonce Knowles' video. Beyonce showed the class Kanye lacked later that night when she won an award and she invited Taylor Swift back up to finish her acceptance speech.

Kanye West has a long history of antisocial behavior. When he failed to win an MTV Europe Award in 2006, he jumped on stage, grabbed the mike from the winner, and explained how his video should have won because it had Pamela Anderson in it and cost $1 million. The following year he complained that MTV opened the show with Britney Spears instead of him because he was black. He left that night infuriated he didn't win a Moonman trophy, vowing never to return. Unfortunately he broke that promise and returned this year, drunk and disorderly.

Oh, and don't forget another classic Kanye moment: during a post-Katrina charity benefit Kanye departed from scripted topics like disaster relief and rebuilding efforts to go on a rambling political diatribe that concluded with the nonsensical generality, "George Bush doesn't care about black people."

Are these the role models of modern society? You're not surprised when a hip-hop thug or a rock star acts outrageous, but we expect better of elected officials. But, as the old saying goes, you can put lipstick on a pig (or Joe Wilson's charcoal suit and power tie) but it's still a pig wearing lipstick.

It's easy to blame this decline in manners on the increased pace of modern life. Everything moves so fast now, there just isn't time for pleasantries like there used to be. But in truth, modern technology makes it even easier to be well-mannered and courteous—no need to buy, write, and mail Thank You notes, when a one-line "Thanks!" email or text message will do.

I think the decline in manners stems from a heightened sense of frustration that grips our nation. The economy stinks, times are hard, and, most importantly, people don't feel like anybody is listening to their complaints and cries for help. If nobody is listening, you start to shout and interrupt. You get rude.

Nowhere is this more evident than in the recent town hall meetings on health care reform. People are worried and frustrated, so they push and shove each other. Even meetings that didn't result in physical altercations got loud and had an air of tension about them. This is rudeness borne of frustration. I suppose Kanye West and Joe Wilson can use the same excuse. But Wilson needs to respect the rules of governing bodies and polite society. And Kanye West needs to get a clue...or, better yet, just get lost.

Joe Wilson's 2009 outburst seems quaint in our current political climate. Donald Trump took rudeness to a new level during the 2016 Presidential Campaign. Kanye West won't go away. He continues to act like an entitled child. Rumor has it Kanye was once laughed at by hip-hop insiders, and has a massive chip on his shoulder. He's proven them all wrong. Now everyone laughs at him.

ROCK STAR OBITUARIES: THE ANTI-DRUG

April 2002

There's a new ad campaign designed to keep kids off drugs that promotes "anti-drug" activities, such as family, friends, sports, music, and art. I'd like to submit my own idea for the anti-drug campaign: the obituary page.

The obituary page is where hardcore drug abusers end up, often much earlier than the rest of their generation. The latest drug casualty to end up on the obit page is Layne Staley, the lead singer of the rock group Alice in Chains. To me, Staley's tale epitomizes just how dark and depressing the life of a drug addict can be.

Drug abuse, namely heroin addiction, has claimed the lives of countless rock musicians. Alice in Chains broke on the music scene in the early '90s. Several contemporaries of Staley's in the alternative music scene are already dead from drug abuse. Nirvana frontman Kurt Cobain shot himself in the midst of a drug-addled depression. Shannon Hoon from Blind Melon and Brad Nowell from Sublime both overdosed. As tragic as it was to see these artists die at the peak of their success (and, in the case of Hoon and Nowell, before they even reached the heights of rock stardom), Staley's story is sadder still.

Alice in Chains stopped touring in 1994 because of Layne's erratic, drugged-out behavior. They were able to record a couple more albums, but they weren't able to tour in support of them. In 1996, Alice in Chains played its last live performance on MTV's Unplugged. Everyone who saw it agreed: Layne looked bad. Staley's last interview was in 1998. He said he was out of drug rehab and was planning some "big things." But nothing big came out of Layne again. He became a recluse, living in his Seattle apartment and getting high. He did this for the next three years.

In April 2002 a relative who hadn't heard from Layne in a few weeks asked police to enter his apartment. They found the 34-year-old singer dead on his couch, heroin needles on the floor beside him. His body was in such a state of decomposition, an autopsy was needed to determine his identity.

Staley's story is perhaps the most powerful anti-drug message. Drug addiction doesn't discriminate between rock stars and regular Joes. Both end up in the graveyard before their time. It's not a peaceful end, either. Staley died forgotten and alone because he drove away everyone who cared about him. I can't think of a more pitiful way to go.

In truth, Layne Staley died years ago. It took until April 2002 until his wasted body finally shut down, but he had been slowly fading away since 1995, maybe earlier. Drugs robbed Staley of his talent, his motivation and, ultimately, his life. He was one of the best singers in rock music, but he died a lonely loser, another dead junkie.

A horrible death is the best anti-drug.

Miss you, Layne. Some days you slay the rooster...some days the rooster slays you.

IS ROBOT-MUSICIAN THE FUTURE OF MUSIC?

May 2010

Shimon rocks!

Shimon is a four-armed marimba-playing robot. What's a marimba? It's an instrument similar to a xylophone; Brian Jones played one on The Rolling Stones' "Under My Thumb."

Shimon isn't the first robot designed to make music. But it might be the first that's able to *improvise* music, and jam along with other musicians through unexpected, and unannounced, chord changes. Shimon relies on complex algorithms to identify tempo, beats, and chord progressions, as well as melodic dissonance and consonance. This allows Shimon to "listen" to music, analyze its structure, and improvise with other musicians. That explains the name: Shimon means "one who hears" or "one who is heard" in Hebrew.

Shimon's stainless steel head looks like a toaster with a blinking camera eye on one end. Shimon looks at other musicians when they solo, and visually acknowledges them as it bobs its toaster-head in time with the music.

Gil Weinberg, director of the Georgia Tech Center for Music Technology, created Shimon two years ago. Ryan Nikolaidis, a PhD student at Georgia Tech, is one of Shimon's programmers. He plays piano while Shimon plays the marimba, each jam session deepening Shimon's musical knowledge and broadening its base of improvisational skills.

"Being able to shift between different influences, and create a rich vocabulary that's nothing like any human would ever play...hopefully this then inspires us to play differently as well, play something that we wouldn't play with other humans," Nikolaidis says.

Is this the next step in musical evolution? Consider the other ways technology has affected music creation and distribution. Sampling, hard disc recording, and digital editing software allow anyone to create music (you don't even need to be a musician), and Autotune gives everyone a passable singing voice. It's about time computers took the knowledge musicians and programmers have fed them for years and produced some original music.

This isn't like the old adage about "giving a monkey a typewriter" and hoping it pounds out Shakespeare. This is like teaching a monkey the basics of grammar, syntax, and composition, letting it read every book ever written, and then giving it a word processor. Unlike your typical typing monkey (hey, no jokes about yours truly!), Shimon should be able to produce music that's actually *listenable*. Shimon composes music not with a human's sensibilities, but with what a machine *thinks* are human sensibilities. It probably won't sound like Lady Gaga, (or maybe it will) but it should be interesting. It might even teach us something new about music.

Plus, Shimon is more reliable than most band mates.

He'll show up at rehearsal on time and won't ever get tired.

He'll never ask for a pay raise or even a smoke break.

He won't quit the band to pursue a solo career.

His skills should improve over time, not deteriorate with age or hard living.

He'll never trash a hotel room, or get arrested for illegal guns, narcotics, or public urination.

You'll never have to make him go to rehab, no, no, no.

He'll avoid complicated romantic entanglements, unless he tries to seduce a microphone stand. ("Hey, she's tall and thin, with a nice, wide bottom!")

He won't "expand his brand," and venture into acting, clothes design, perfume and/or jewelry manufacturing, blogging, reality television, or politics.

Most importantly, he won't overdose, choke on his own vomit, or drown in a swimming pool (short circuit, maybe). He won't die young, so like many promising musicians. He won't be susceptible to depression and self-indulgence. Given the ever-learning nature of Shimon's programming, he should continue to grow and develop as an artist. Shimon, and the musical robots destined to follow him, may some day carry mankind's musical knowledge on to Earth's next inhabitants.

Shimon, you crazy diamond!

Soul music created by the soulless for the soulless—neo-robo soul. Shimon is the music of tomorrow, today.

WU-TANG CLAN OFFERS MUSIC INDUSTRY A NEW BUSINESS MODEL

December 2015

Rap/hip-hop pioneers Wu-Tang Clan are still blazing new trails in the music industry, this time with an inventive business strategy that sounds like the punch-line to a bad joke: The band released a new album, but it only sold one copy. Luckily, somebody paid $2 million for it.

Wu-Tang Clan recently auctioned off the one-and-only edition of its new album, *Once Upon A Time in Shaolin*, for $2 million. *Once Upon A Time in Shaolin* was produced last year, and features 31 tracks, and a leather-bound 174-page book of lyrics and liner notes.

Wu-Tang producer/performer, RZA, described the album as "a piece of art like nobody else had done in the history of music. We're making a single–sale collector's item. This is like someone having the scepter of an Egyptian king."

According to RZA, the album attracted many suitors: "Private collectors, trophy hunters, millionaires, billionaires, unknown folks, publicly known folks, businesses, companies with commercial intent, young, old," he said. Filmmaker Quentin Tarantino and venture capitalist Ben Horowitz allegedly expressed interest in buying the album.

Who was the winning bidder? Villainous pharmaceutical executive Martin Shkreli, who made headlines earlier this year for jacking up the price of a drug used to treat AIDS from $13.50 per pill to $750 per pill. *Boo!* Nobody likes to see the Bad Guy win!

The sale was finalized May 2015, long before Shkreli's public display of greed at the expense of AIDS patients. Even so, Wu-Tang claims it will donate a large part of its $2 million payday to charity.

Despite its despicable new owner, *Once Upon A Time in Shaolin* sets a new precedent in the music business. Once upon a time in rock 'n' roll, musical artists toured in order to sell albums. Commercial radio, the original "free music service," helped by promoting shows and playing singles.

But free digital downloads offer no such reciprocal relationship. Digital music takes that revenue stream away, forcing artists to recoup their loses through touring and merchandise sales. That's why concerts tickets now cost $400, and t-shirts nearly $100.

Wu-Tang Clan has introduced an intriguing twist to the idea of "collectible merchandise." Artists from Radiohead to Louis CK have successfully experimented with direct-to-fan sales in recent years. Perhaps Wu-Tang's "direct-to-fan" high-bidder album is the next step in the evolution of modern music marketing.

It will be interesting to see what Shkreli does with his new prize. Re-sell it for a tidy profit, probably. But Wu-Tang Clan's rare record sale inspires new possibilities in the business relationship between artists and fans. What could top a personalized album from your favorite musical artist? How much for Paul McCartney to write me a theme song?

In 2015, Martin Shkreli was found guilty of securities fraud and sentenced to seven years in prison. Once Upon A Time in Shaolin *was seized by the federal government, along with the rest of Shkreli's assets. He doesn't even have a cool album to listen to while he serves his time. Karma is a wheel.*

CELEBRITY ADOPTIONS ARE AN ORPHAN'S LOTTERY

November 2006

People look to celebrities for cues on how to live their lives. They buy the products celebrities endorse, they decorate their homes like celebrity homes, dress the same, vacation in the same resorts. Celebrity culture shapes popular opinion, in everything from fashion to politics. Sad, shallow, but true.

So when Madonna adopts a 13-month-old baby named David Banda from the African nation of Malawi, she's setting an example. Critics lambasted the Material Girl for her quick Third World adoption. Some questioned the sincerity of it, others the legality. Certain human rights groups have alleged that Madonna used her fame and fortune to circumvent Malawi's adoption laws. Others feared Madonna's Malawi adoption would open the door for slave traffickers—a far-fetched notion to say the least.

I admire what Madonna did. I admire anyone who adopts a child. There are far too many children in this world who need good homes. There is not enough love to go around, it seems. And frankly, David Banda could do far worse than having Madonna as a mother. Sure, she's a freaky Momma—an autoworker's daughter who grew up in the suburbs of Detroit, who, thanks to superstardom, has recast herself as an English princess. But David Banda will want for nothing growing up, and he'll be afforded every opportunity in life. He'll probably grow up with a whole set of problems being Madonna's son, but they'll be much more benign than the ones he would have faced in his native land—starvation, lack of education, menial labor, and death from a preventable disease. First World Problems aren't so bad.

My wife and I were Adoption Counselors at the local animal shelter for many years. We would screen people who came in looking to adopt a dog and then approve or deny the adoption. Most of the people who came into the shelter were what you'd call "shoppers"—they had been to other shelters, maybe even the pet shop down at the mall, and they were looking for a very specific type of dog to add to their family. We made some good matches this way, but if you didn't have the dog they were looking for, they weren't interested in any of the others.

But occasionally you'd get an individual or family who came in looking for a dog, any dog, who needed a good home. They'd have pictures of their other dogs, past and present; usually pictured sleeping on their couches or splashing in the family pool. They'd have vet bills and medical references showing how they cared for their pets. These families were golden, and we'd always introduce them to our hard-luck cases; the animals who had been there the longest or had health problems. More often than not they'd end up going home with one—or two—of our harder-to-place pets. Afterwards my wife and I would toast each other and say, "That dog just hit the Doggie Lottery!" Truly these were rags-to-riches stories.

David Banda hit the human equivalent of the Doggie Lottery, the Orphan's Lottery, as it were. So have the adopted children of Angelina Jolie and Brad Pitt, actor Ewan McGregor and his wife, Mia Farrow, Julie Andrews, and other Hollywood hotshots who have pursued international adoptions. These children were plucked from Third World poverty and put on the fast-track to a life of luxury.

And if others are inspired to open their homes to Third World children based on the actions of Madonna and Jolie, that's all the better. Celebrities are actually setting a good example for a change, endorsing a cause—the plight of needy children—that we should all support.

Madonna adopted four children from Malawi, and all appear to be semi-normal. David Banda is 12 and enjoys soccer. His Mom even moved him to Lisbon, Portugal so he could train with professional players. Madge is the ultimate soccer mom!

EXPOSING BOOB TUBE HYPOCRISY

February 2004

Grown men cried. Women fainted. Children were traumatized for life. The American psyche was forever scarred.

No, terrorist attacks or wartime anxiety didn't cause this mental angst. It can't be blamed on an upswing in unemployment or a downward economy. It's all because Janet Jackson bared her breast during the Super Bowl Half-Time Show.

Even now, several weeks after Janet (Ms. Jackson if you're nasty) and Justin Timberlake's ill-conceived publicity stunt went awry, the repercussions are still being felt. The FCC is investigating the entire half-time show. A Tennessee woman is suing, claiming that she, along with millions of other television viewers, are owed monetary damages for exposure to lewd conduct. CBS, which produced the Super Bowl, blames MTV, which produced the Half-Time Show. America Online, which sponsored the whole thing, is demanding a refund.

Hypocrisy abounds here. For starters, CBS, the nation's

most conservative network, and MTV, the nation's raunchiest, are both owned by media mega-corp, Viacom. They have no one to blame but themselves. And "family friendly" Internet provider America Online's cries of moral outrage are laughable; AOL-Time Warner is one of the biggest traffickers of pornography in this country. They pump it through the Internet, sell it as part of their cable packages, and deliver it to newsstands all over the globe.

The media was quick to condemn Janet for exposing her breast during a "family-friendly" event like the Super Bowl, exposing children to unseemly sexual behavior. Yet they took Ms. Jackson's two-second "wardrobe malfunction" and replayed it over and over again at all hours of the day and night. If your kid missed Janet's boob flash during the Super Bowl, he or she was sure to catch it again on the news, most likely in slow-mo and/or freeze frame.

Finally, the public outcry over this episode was ridiculous. What's the difference between what Janet Jackson revealed at the Super Bowl and what professional cheerleaders reveal on the sidelines of every NFL game? Less than a square inch of wispy fabric is my guess. And how "family-friendly" is the Super Bowl anyway? It's a game of giant men giving each other brain injuries, and every other commercial is pushing beer or prescription drugs. What kind of message does that send?

The only person who wasn't damaged by Janet's antics is Janet herself. She has a new album coming out, and a little extra "exposure" isn't a bad thing.

Warriors clash on the battlefield while scantily clad women cheer from the sidelines…it's like a Frank Frazetta painting! Sports are a wonderfully stupid waste of time!

Sport Geeks

SPORTS ARE STUPID

January 2019

Wait…what did I just say about the Super Bowl in that last column?

"It's a game of giant men giving each other brain injuries, and every other commercial is pushing beer or prescription drugs."

No way! The Super Bowl is America's greatest sporting event!

Yes, but it's still a dumb, dangerous game. Science has proven the dangers of football, but it's going to take a while before the rest of us accept it.

Sports, in general, are a waste of time, but entertaining as hell. Go Yanks!

READY FOR SOME FOOTBALL? HOW ABOUT DOMESTIC VIOLENCE?

September 2014

Americans love violence. We love it in our music, movies, and TV shows. Even our cartoons are violent. Violence is entertaining! I'm no different. I'm a proud American—I love violent entertainment, too!

We enjoy violent sports. Let the rest of the world call soccer "football"; every red-blooded American knows "real" football is about giant men suiting up in pads and helmets— like ancient knights going into battle—and crashing into each other at top speed. Bone-crushing hits. Backbreaking tackles. Devastating sacks. That's football!

Football is a violent game played by violent men. While most professional football players leave their aggression on the field, some bring their work home with them. A brief look at NFL history reveals its violent legacy.

Most recently, Baltimore Ravens running back Ray Rice was suspended after punching out his wife (then fiancée) in an elevator. Current Cincinnati Bengals cornerback Adam "Pac-Man" Jones was in countless altercations (usually at strip clubs) including a shooting that left a man paralyzed. Jets quarterback Michael Vick served 23 months in jail for animal abuse and running an illegal dogfighting ring. New England Patriots tight end Aaron Hernandez is currently being held without bail on charges he murdered three men. [*Author's Note: Not anymore. Aaron Hernandez hung himself to death in his jail cell after being found guilty of murder.*]

Gridiron great Jim Brown was arrested several times for assaulting and threatening women. Rams/Dolphins running back Lawrence Phillips was sentenced in 2009 to 31 years in prison after assaulting his girlfriend and driving his car into three teenagers. Baltimore Ravens linebacker (and current ESPN commentator) Ray Lewis was involved in a brawl that left two men stabbed to death.

Rae Carruth, former wide receiver for the Carolina Panthers, had his pregnant girlfriend killed in 2001, and is serving an 18-24 year sentence for his crime. When former Seattle Seahawks wide receiver Tommy Kane's wife told him she wanted a divorce in November 2003, he dragged her into the kitchen, smashed her head on the floor, and stabbed her in the neck. He was charged with second degree murder, but pled guilty to manslaughter.

Buffalo Bills defensive tackle Jim Dunaway fractured his ex-wife's skull, and then tossed her lifeless body into a swimming pool in 1998. While he was never charged with murder, he was found guilty in a wrongful death suit filed by his children. Coincidentally, Dunaway played on the Bills with superstar running back O.J. Simpson for three seasons. And O.J…well, you know.

Current Minnesota Vikings running back Adrian Peterson is

a child abuser (though he claims he was "just disciplining" his four-year-old son when he beat him bloody with a tree branch). Ironically, Peterson was in the news 11 months ago when his two-year-old son—a child Peterson never knew he had—was beaten to death by the child's mother's boyfriend. You'd think Peterson might back off corporal punishment for his surviving children after this incident. You'd be wrong.

The NFL's "culture of violence" is more than a media buzz-phrase, it's the nature of the sport (same as boxing and UFC/MMA fights). But football's off-field aggression has reached a boiling point.

James Naddeo writes on SportsGrid.com, "All of these instances have brought about an existential crisis for both the NFL and its fans. The NFL has reached a crossroads of sorts, where they need to define what exactly they stand for."

The NFL is taking domestic violence seriously. NFL Commissioner Roger Goodell announced he's working with four women "on the development and implementation of the league's policies, resources, and outreach on issues of domestic violence and sexual assault." Maybe the league needs to make the game more about speed, grace, and tactical play rather than bone-crushing brawn.

After all, violence is only part of what makes football so great. Yes, it's fun watching big men get knocked down. ("The bigger they are, the harder they fall!") But watching them get back up and do it again the next play is what makes a champion. That's what heroes do; get knocked down and rise back up. That's football at its best, pushing the boundaries of skill and endurance, and celebrating the triumph and determination of the human spirit.

But football at its worst is about permanent brain injury. Come on, people, some of these players aren't working with much to begin with!

FAKE VERB ENTERS REAL DISCUSSION ON CATFISHED JOCK

February 2013

"Manti Te'o got catfished!"

Wait...who got what?

Manti Te'o is a senior at Notre Dame University, one of the most decorated collegiate football players of all time. And "getting catfished" means he fell victim to an apparent hoax, specifically, a fake girlfriend he met on the Internet.

Why should you care? You shouldn't. The guy made a dumb mistake, a mistake I'm sure he wishes he could keep private. But when you're a sports star (or anyone else in the ever-expanding pool of "public figures") you lose that privacy—especially when you start discussing your imaginary girlfriend on national television.

But the Manti Te'o story is interesting for other reasons. First, what does it say about our nation's college and

145

high school sports programs when an apparent knucklehead like Manti Te'o can graduate high school with a 3.5 GPA, and "earn" full scholarships to over 30 of America's top universities? If you're looking for the sharpest tool in the shed, Manti Te'o is a rubber mallet.

Is Manti Te'o a good example of a Notre Dame education? Or was Te'o—like so many college athletes— handed a diploma without actually having to learn anything in college? How is that fair to people who not only pay for college themselves, but earn the grades, too?

The Manti Te'o story is the first time the word "catfish" has been introduced as a verb in the mass media. This strange term comes from the 2010 independent film called *Catfish*, a supposed documentary directed by Henry Joost and Ariel Schulman, about Ariel's brother Nev's relationship with a 19-year-old girl he meets on Facebook. When Nev pays the girl a surprise visit to meet her in person, he finds his dream girl is actually a frumpy middle-aged woman who cares for several disabled children. The woman's blue-collar husband delivers an anecdote that gives the movie its title.

According to her husband, vats of live cod were once shipped from Alaska to China, but the meat was mushy and tasteless by the time the fish reached its destination. Someone had the idea to put catfish in the tank, to chase the cod around and keep them active, that way the meat would taste fresher.

"I thank god for the catfish," Hubby says. "Because life would be drab, boring and dull if you didn't have someone nipping at your fins."

It's an interesting idea, and a nice analogy for the film—Nev and his friends are the unwitting cods, and the frumpy housewife is the catfish, keeping them alert, keeping them guessing.

But it's not accurate. Most Internet scammers aren't "playing with you" out of boredom or loneliness. They want to hack your bank account, steal your identity, or worse. A real catfish is not a "colorful motivator." That's your spouse. A real catfish wants to steal something from you.

But it turns out the fishy story that gives *Catfish* its name is also false. There's no evidence live cod were ever shipped from Alaska to China, no evidence catfish were put into the tanks to keep them active. It's all a lie. Henry Joost and Ariel Schulman wrote the lines, and an actor read them, which makes you question the legitimacy of the rest of their "documentary."

So, the next time you hear someone got "catfished," know it's a fake verb, inspired by a fake story, from a fake documentary, about fake people on the Internet. Maybe the quadruple layer of deception adds detail to this description of a truly modern dilemma.

Just don't ask Manti Te'o to explain it.

Poor Manti! He is another victim of the Racist World Of Sports!

Rob Errera

LADY GOLFERS TEED OFF AT ENGLISH-ONLY RULE

September 2008

"To continue in English, please press one. *Para seguir en Español, oprima el numero dos.*"

It's a common refrain, one that anyone who calls a customer service number anywhere is familiar with. But you won't hear it if you call the front offices of the Ladies Professional Golf Association. You won't be given the option to continue your call in Chinese, Japanese, Korean, Italian, Greek, or Hindu either. It's English only at the LPGA.

The LPGA will require players to speak English during pro-am tournaments, trophy presentations, and media interviews starting in 2009, with players who have been LPGA members for two years facing suspension if they can't pass an "oral evaluation" of English skills. The rule is effective immediately for new players. There are 121 international players from 26 countries on the LPGA Tour, including 45 players from South Korea.

The LPGA ruling is a controversial move, one that appears to be blatantly discriminatory toward the influx of Asian golfers who have become so highly ranked in the sport. But the LPGA claims the English-only rule is an unfortunate result of economics.

Unlike some professional sports, the LPGA has so significant television sponsorship or corporate backing. Instead, its main source of funding is a series of pro-am tournaments where sponsors get a chance to golf a round with the game's top ranked female players. More and more frequently the scenario is, a private or corporate sponsor spends $50,000-plus to golf with a South Korean player who can't communicate with them beyond smiles and nods. It's not making anyone feel warm and fuzzy, and it's got the LPGA worried about losing sponsors.

"Unlike athletes in other sports, LPGA players must entertain and engage sponsors and their customers on a weekly basis; our business model does not rely on advertising and ticket sales as others do," said LPGA Commissioner Carolyn F. Bivens. "Before these players tee it up for a tournament, they play in pro-ams spending 5-6 hours with the sponsors and guests. No other sport gives fans and sponsors this kind of direct access and experience. Not surprisingly, sponsors pay a lot of money to play with our pros. Sponsors also end up developing individual business relationships with the pros they play with. It is imperative for the future success of the LPGA as well as the success of each LPGA player that our members effectively communicate in English at tournaments inside the United States with those who provide for the existence of the tournaments."

Therein lies the problem for the LPGA; it's not looking for the best players in the sport, it's looking for the best players/spokesmodels/sales reps. It doesn't want the best female golfers; it wants the best "entertaining and engaging" female golfers. It cheapens the integrity of the sport, to the point where you have to question if the Ladies Professional Golf Association is really "professional" at all. The English Speaking American Women's Golf Association is a more appropriate name, but it doesn't roll off the tongue right, and ESAWGA looks bad in print.

Sports are not professional if you restrict players based on language or ethnicity (which some say are inseparable), religious beliefs, skin color, etc. That's called discrimination. Imagine if professional boxing became English-speaking only. Would there be anyone left to fight?

And the LPGA's English-only policy sets a terrible double standard. Last year's winner of the U.S. Open, Angel Cabrera, is from Argentina and conducted all of his post-trophy interviews through a Spanish interpreter. The best female golfers in the world should be given that same opportunity.

But, at the other end of the multi-lingual spectrum, consider the birthday party held for New York Yankees outfielder Hideki Matsui this summer. Matsui is one of the biggest stars in Japanese baseball and a troop of Japanese reporters follow his every move here in the United States. He has played in New York since 2003 and will have earned more than $75 million before his contract expires after the 2009 season.

So the Yankees organization rolls out a cake to celebrate his 34th birthday and, after a few introductory speeches, the cameras turn to Matsui who steps up to the mike and says simply, "Thank you." There's an awkward pause as they wait for him to say more, but he doesn't. He smiles and nods. The cameras flash. Working in a city for over five years, earning $75 million, and the best you can manage in the native tongue is "Thank You"? Lame. (It's worth noting, however, that Matsui also hit a grand slam on his 34th birthday, driving in all four runs in a 4-in-1 victory over Oakland…underscoring the fact that he is paid to play baseball, not speak English.)

Most professional athletes in the United States understand the importance of speaking passable English, if not for the sake of communicating better with fellow players, then for media interviews and endorsement deals. (Sure, you might land some print ads, but you're not going to get that lucrative underarm deodorant commercial unless you "speaka da English.") But *demanding* players speak English? That's not playing fair.

I told you racism runs rampant in professional sports! Team owners are greedy too!

GREAT SEATS SIT EMPTY AT NEW YANKEE STADIUM

May 2010

I haven't been to the new Yankee Stadium yet. I'd like to take my wife and kids out for a day at the ballpark, but I figure it will probably cost me at least 500 bucks after tickets, parking, food, and souvenirs. Maybe I'll have the extra cash later in the season, though chances are better I'll be asked to replace Derek Jeter in the line-up.

But I see a problem at the new Yankee stadium, a problem that was evident last year, during the stadium's inaugural season, and appears to have gotten worse.

The problem is empty seats.

It looks like the stands are half empty at Yankee home games. A big chunk of prime seats behind home plate and along the baselines are vacant. I know it's early in the season, but come on! These are the defending World Series Champs, and it looks like the crowd at one of my daughter's T-ball games!

The camera shots are deceptive, though. When the camera pans back, you can see the middle tier and upper deck are filled. But the best seats in the house remain empty.

The Yankees priced these seats too high. Prices were originally between $500-$2500 for these premium seats. I hear those prices have been cut in half, but they are still outrageous. Another problem is corporate season ticket holders who, for whatever reason, leave good seats unused. These empty seats aren't only a waste of space, they make the entire team look unsupported and amateurish.

Major League Baseball should look to the Oscars and other awards shows for a solution. The answer is professional seat-fillers. When a star at an awards show wants to duck out for a smoke or bathroom break, a well dressed, good-looking, ultra-attentive "seat-filler" takes their place until they return. This way, when the camera pans the audience, it always looks like the place is packed.

The Yankees should get a crew of professional seat-fillers together to occupy these empty seats. Dress attractive people in official Yankee gear, and sit them behind home plate— you've got a living advertisement on camera every pitch of the game. The seat-fillers should be in place by the start of the game, and if the official ticket holder shows up (hey, it's not uncommon to hit traffic around the stadium), the seat-filler gives them the seat.

But if the absent ticket-holders don't show by the end of the fifth inning, the Yankees should raffle the vacant seats off to people sitting out in the bleachers or up in the nosebleed section. Let a true fan watch the rest of the game from a great seat. That would be a nice giveback to the fans who paid for lesser seats.

But what about fans who paid for expensive seats? Won't they get upset? Perhaps, but they get to watch the entire game from a premium seat. The lucky seat-lottery winner only gets to watch the last few innings. Expensive Seat Fan should be angry at himself/herself for spending several thousand dollars on tickets to a baseball game.

A premium seat lottery would be fun for viewers at home, too. ("Hey, wasn't there a cute blonde in a W.B. Mason t-shirt sitting behind home plate last inning? Why is a fat drunk with a pinstripe-painted face in her seat?")

I'm sure those empty seats cost the corporate ticket-holders and the Yankee organization quite a bit of money. These highly visible no-shows also reflect poorly on the team itself. It looks like the 27-time World Champions can't draw a crowd to their brand-new stadium.

Looking at it from a dollars-and-cents angle (and you'd hope the team with the biggest payroll in the Major Leagues is watching its bottom line), these wasted seats not only demonstrate an underwhelming display of team support, they're also a waste of potential advertising space.

Great seats still sit empty at Yankee Stadium. So far, no one has thought to toss seat-fillers—or mannequins—in those seats wearing Coca-Cola t-shirts, and other branded merchandise. Soon…

BARRY BONDS A RECORD-BREAKER, SPIRIT KILLER

June 2006

Barry Bonds broke Babe Ruth's career home run record…and the spirit of baseball fans everywhere.

On paper, Barry Bonds is one of the greatest players of all time. He won a record seven MVP awards over the course of his career. He is the only player in baseball history to have hit at least 500 home runs and stolen at least 500 bases (no other player has reached even 400-400). Bonds won eight Gold Glove Awards for his defensive prowess in left field, and he is a 13-time All-Star. And now he is the second highest home run hitter in history, shattering Ruth's record and trailing his idol Hank Aaron by less than 40 homers.

But Bonds is a cheat, repeatedly linked to steroid use. While other major league players have come forward and admitted using performance enhancing drugs, Bonds will only say that he "never knowingly" used them.

155

Even his own teammates don't believe him, and most don't like him. He's anti-social in the clubhouse, frequently refusing to talk to his teammates. His relationship with the press isn't much better. His interviews are often cantankerous and when something is printed he doesn't like—which is often—Bonds will claim he was misquoted.

One of the most glaring examples of this occurred during a 2003 press conference when he maligned Babe Ruth's legacy.

"The only number I'm concerned with is Babe Ruth's," Bonds said. "As a left-handed hitter, I wiped him out. That's it. And in the baseball world, Babe Ruth is everything, right? I got his (single season) slugging percentage, I got him on on-base, I got him on walks and then I'll take his (lifetime) home run record and that's it. Don't talk about him no more."

It's interesting to note that when Ruth started out in the big leagues, baseball was still reeling from the 1919 Black Sox scandal. (The Chicago White Sox intentionally lost the World Series.) People were disillusioned with the sport of baseball, its popularity at an all-time low. America's national pastime was in danger of extinction.

But Ruth's dynamic performances on the field—and his gregarious personality off the field—won over a whole new generation of fans. People got excited about going to the ballpark again. In short, Babe Ruth almost single-handedly saved baseball from extinction.

Barry Bonds did the opposite. He turned untold numbers of people off to baseball. He mired the sport in controversy and scandal. He shattered a bunch of records during his career, but can you really call someone so unscrupulous, so self-centered, a "great player"?

There's comfort knowing there are still some records Bonds is unlikely to break; Babe Ruth still has nearly 100 wins as a pitcher under his belt.

Better work on your knuckleball, Barry.

Barry Bonds is a dick. So is Mark McGwire.

Rob Errera

MCGWIRE APOLOGY TOO LITTLE, TOO LATE, TOO LAME

January 2010

The old saying goes, "It's never too late to say you're sorry."

However...

Most apologies come with a sell-by date. If you go too far past it, things start to stink really bad.

One of the most recent—and perhaps most obnoxious—examples of the pungent apology came courtesy of home run hero Mark McGwire. McGwire held the record for most home runs during a single season, knocking 70 balls out of the park in 1998. That was a wild year for baseball, with McGwire and Sammy Sosa in a record-breaking home run race. McGwire finished the season with a record-setting 70 homers, but Sosa also shattered Roger Maris' single season record that year with 66 homers. Barry Bonds currently holds the single season home run record; he smacked 73 homers in 2001.

However…

All of these records have been tainted by the use of steroids and other performance-enhancing drugs. Bonds tested positive for using steroids, but claimed he didn't know what his trainer gave him. Sosa also tested positive for steroid use; he also used an illegal "corked" bat to swat homers out of the park. And now McGwire has come forward to apologize for using steroids, more than a decade after his record-breaking season.

McGwire's *mea culpa* stunk up the joint for a number of reasons. For starters, the shelf life had long expired on this apology. McGwire enjoyed the benefits of being a Home Run King for more than a decade before telling the truth. He had plenty of opportunities to come clean before this, especially during the Congressional investigation into steroid use in MLB several years back. But he didn't.

And each time another player was implicated with steroid use, McGwire passed up a chance to come clean himself. Jose Canseco, Gary Sheffield, Rafael Palmeiro, Jason Giambi; the Forgiveness Factor seems to depend entirely on the depth of involvement coupled with a quick and sincere apology. Those who only used steroids briefly and apologized quickly—like pitcher Andy Pettitte—got a lighter sentence in the court of public opinion. Those who denied, denied, denied and then got busted—like Alex Rodriguez—were judged more harshly. McGwire's apology was simply too little, too late, and too lame.

Still, McGwire's apology might end up smelling like a rose compared to those players who still haven't come clean about their steroid use. Roger Clemens continues to deny using performance enhancing drugs, despite evidence to the contrary. The biggest phony of all is MLB manager Tony La Russa. Some of the biggest offenders of steroid use in baseball have played on La Russa's teams. He managed Canseco, McGwire, and Giambi as rookies while overseeing the Oakland A's and the St. Louis Cardinals. La Russa didn't stop denying Canseco used steroids until Canseco published his autobiography, *Juiced*. La Russa has always denied McGwire's steroid use, too. Sure, Tony. Pull the other leg; it plays "Jingle Bells."

Perhaps the most honorable thing for MLB to do now would be to return the single season home run record back to the family of Roger Maris; Maris bested Babe Ruth's 34-year record by hitting 61 homers back in 1961. Maris' record stood for 37 years; then in the span of three years, 1998-2001, three 'roid-heads toppled him. It hardly seems fair. It's unlikely McGwire, Sosa, and Bonds would have been able to accomplish what they did without the use of performance-enhancing drugs.

It's never too late to say you're sorry. It's not too late to fix mistakes and set the record straight, either.

Grown men paid millions to play a little boy's game…and they still find a way to cheat! Minor league players would cut their arms off to play in the majors! But that's a bad idea. Cutting your arm off is almost always a bad idea…

A ONE-ARMED LESSON IN BRAVERY

May 2003

Aron Ralston, 27, of Aspen, CO is an excellent climber. Over the years he has scaled 49 of Colorado's major peaks. When he set out on a recent Saturday morning to climb the walls of Blue John Canyon near Canyonlands National Park on the border of Utah and Colorado, he was anticipating another thrilling outdoor adventure.

He got more than he bargained for. Much more.

A 200-pound boulder rolled down the mountainside, crushing Ralston's hand and pinning him to the mountain.

He waited for help. None came. On Tuesday, three days later, Ralston ran out of water. By Thursday morning he knew he would die alone on the mountainside if he didn't do something drastic. So he did.

Ralston used a pocketknife to amputate his own arm just below the elbow. He wrapped a tourniquet around the wound to stop the bleeding. Then he rigged anchors, fixed a

161

rope, and rappelled to the canyon floor.

Ralston hiked downstream and was spotted about 3 p.m. Thursday afternoon by a Utah Public Safety Helicopter. The search for Ralston began that morning, after authorities learned he was four days overdue reporting for work.

I'm not sure if Aron Ralston's story is one of great bravery or great stupidity. Maybe a little of both. It certainly raises questions, like, why would Ralston climb a mountain by himself? He was an experienced climber, surely he heard of the "buddy system"? Why go hiking alone without a mobile phone, a two-way radio, or some other way to signal for help if, let's say, a boulder falls on you?

Ralston might have died if he hadn't taken steps to save himself. Ironically, he might have also been saved—both arms intact—if he had hung in there a few more hours. The search for him had only started that morning. But Aron Ralston did what he thought he had to do.

Perhaps the big lesson here is about the resilience of the human spirit and the will to survive. In a day and age when it seems half the populace is on anti-depressant medication and the other half is reading self-help books, it's refreshing to hear about someone like Ralston, who clearly enjoys living life and pushing it to its extremes. This guy's no whining, self-pitying couch potato. In fact, Ralston will probably slap on a prosthetic hand and be back on the hiking trails within a month. He seems like that type of guy, full of courage and bravery.

Still, I can't help but think he wouldn't have needed to be so brave if he had only used his brain a bit first.

Why do I shit on this brave man? Maybe because I'm not an outdoorsman. Hiking frightens me. I'm an AV Club Dweeb!

AV Club Dweeb

PORTRAIT OF THE GEEK AS A YOUNG MAN

January 2019

I was part of the Audio/Video Club in grade school, but I'd grown too cool for film projectors by high school. It wasn't rock 'n' roll enough. But my love of science and technology never waned—I'm a geek for life!

Rob Errera

COMPUTER GEEKS INHERIT THE EARTH

February 1997

The Bible says the meek shall inherit the earth, but I think there's a misprint. It should read, the "geeks" shall inherit the earth—namely "computer geeks."

You remember the computer geeks from school—they were the students who ran the film projectors in class, and hung out in the electronics lab. They were routinely bullied by the brawny, brainless school athletes.

Today, those hapless geeks—led by their spiritual gurus, Bill Gates and Steve Jobs—have revolutionized the world, bringing us technological advances like laptop computers and the World Wide Web. The changes they have wrought are so far reaching, they've even altered the meaning of the English language.

In the "old" days, the lowly @ symbol used to only appear in business ledgers and supermarkets, as in "four artichokes @ $5" (wow—expensive artichokes!). Today, because of the computer geek revolution, @ is almost universally accepted

166

as "at," as in "geek@computer.com." The overly hip use of @ has even made its way into the world of marketing, such as "Watch the X-Files, Sunday@9 p.m." Artichoke sales will never be the same.

"Comp-geeks" are also responsible for a variety of bizarre symbols called "smileys." A typical smiley would look like :-) for example. If you don't get it, rotate this page 90 degrees to the right and look it again. Looks like a smiley face, right? Perhaps you're beginning to understand why the computer geeks were beat up so often in high school.

The smiley has several mutations.

:-(means "sad."

: -0 means "surprised."

: -D means "I'm laughing at you."

My personal favorite is *:-(which is a guy with a hunk of jagged metal stuck in his head. (I made this one up, but hey, if computer geeks can do it, why can't I?)

Even the staid world of mathematics is not safe from the computer geek revolution. The simple greater than/less than symbols (remember those, < >?) have been redubbed "carrots," and are an essential building block in the coding of World Wide Web pages.

Is nothing sacred? Of course not. Just ask the guy who originally predicted the meek would inherit the earth >; -)> (devilish wink).

That's right, kids, back in the day we had to use common keyboard characters to create emojis. We couldn't just send animated piles of shit to our friends! Hard times, children! Hard times!

NO DIGITAL ORGANIZER FOR AN ANALOG LIFE

September 2003

Maybe it's a sign of old age, or perhaps my life has gotten more complicated, but I'm not as organized as I used to be.

Once upon a time I used to catalogue all the books in my library both alphabetically and by subject. I used the same system to file my CD collection. Now my library is a jumbled assortment of books and magazines perched preciously on shelves, old science fiction novels rubbing covers with *Parents* magazine and *The Old Farmers Almanac*. My CD collection is spread out over two shelves: A-M on top, N-Z on the bottom. That's as close to order as my life gets these days.

My memory isn't what it used to be either, so I've taken to writing myself notes at night, reminders of things I need to do the next day; go to the bank, buy milk, pay phone bill before they shut off service, etc. I write on yellow sticky Post-It notes, and paste them on my wallet where I'm sure to see them in the morning. Sometimes I'll have five or six notes pasted there, and my wallet looks like a strange bug, shedding yellow scales. Post-It notes decorate my desk at work, too, stuck all around my computer, creating a pale yellow mane around the screen. I toss them out when chores are completed, add more when new things come up. It's how I keep my life on track.

But maybe there's a better way. Maybe I need a PDA.

A PDA is a personal data assistant, basically a fancy version of the electronic organizers and address books that have been around for years. These handheld computers can access email, surf the Web, take pictures, serve as cell phones, and make you look really important while waiting in line for the bus or train. A friend describes how he uses his.

"It's hot-synched up to my computer so I download the news every morning and read it on the train on my way to work," he said. "It updates all the info in my address book along with my desktop computer, too."

Although I'm a big fan of techno gadgets, I'm usually the last guy to buy one. I'm also incredibly cheap—an unfortunate side effect of being incredibly broke. I checked out PDAs in Staples the other day and was tempted to buy one. I could use a PDA to maximize the hours I spend commuting each day, I could rid my desk (and wallet) of sticky notes, and I could set up reminders so I wouldn't keep forgetting everyone's birthday. It sounded appealing until I looked at the price. A cheap PDA costs 100 bucks, a nice one costs much more.

I ended up in the stationery aisle. I picked up a pack of sticky notes, a couple of small spiral notebooks, a pen, and a new address book. (I seem to go through these every few years— my family and friends move around and change phone numbers frequently.) The bill was a little over ten dollars. It may not look pretty, but I'll be able to store and manage the same amount of information as I could have with a PDA at a fraction of the price.

What about downloading the news to read on my morning commute? Well, if I feel like a big spender I can buy a newspaper (between a quarter and fifty cents daily). Of course, reading the paper over the shoulder of the guy sitting in front of me is cheaper yet, saving me another couple dollars a week. If I keep this up, I may be able to afford that PDA by the end of next year.

I'm glued to my smartphone. It's more than a personal assistant. It's a business partner and friend…entertaining too!

IPOD THEREFORE I AM

October 2008

My ear buds were dying.

I was midway through my morning commute when the left speaker cut out. I jiggled the wire and it came back for a few minutes, but by the time I got to work I was down to one channel again. I'd have to pick up a new pair on my lunch break. Going without my iPod for the commute home was not an option.

I'm a Johnny Come Really Lately when it comes to digital music. I didn't own an iPod until last year, but now that I have one, I'm addicted to it. In fact, I'd say my iPod has not only reawakened my musical spirit, it has quietly changed my life in some rather profound ways.

I've always been a music lover (as well as a knock-around musician) but somewhere around the turn of the millennium the music all but stopped for me. My band had dissolved, and life tossed other priorities my way—a home renovation, a marriage, and then kids. Once kids were on the scene, my

171

main source of musical entertainment was Baby Einstein and
Sesame Street. If we wanted to rock hard, we'd put on *The
Wiggles.*

Yeah, I had a cabinet filled with hundreds of CDs, but when
was I going to listen to them? In the middle of the night
when the kids were asleep? During the ten-minute ride from
my house to the bus stop?

I resisted the iPod craze for a long time. I'd never been a
"Walkman guy," either the cassette tape or CD versions, and
the whole iPod/MP3 player thing seemed like an extension
of that. Lack of space finally nudged me into the digital age; I
needed to clear out my CD cabinet to make room for
computer equipment. So I started the long process of
importing my CD collection into iTunes and I picked up a
used iPod shuffle on eBay.

I was immediately hooked. For starters I could load 17 hours
of music onto a device the size of a matchbook. And the
sound was awesome. Nothing beats listening to music on
headphones, which block out ambient sound and allow you
to hear every nuance of the music. I'm sure music purists
will disagree, but a good pair of "ear buds" put music *inside*
your head in a way that standard headphones never can
(especially not those cheesy, foam-eared, Walkman-style
headphones). When was the last time I listened to music on
headphones? In college? High school?

I didn't realize how much I missed listening to music—not
watching music videos, but *listening* to music—until I got an
iPod. It felt like a cool drink on a hot summer day. It was
more than merely refreshing. It was like getting something
back that was crucial to my well-being, a vitamin missing
from my diet.

My iPod quickly transformed my dreary New York City
commute into an almost enjoyable experience. If it's a rainy
day and the subway platforms are dank and crowded, you're

going to need some Metallica or Tool to make it through. Nothing beats checking out the celestial paintings on the ceiling of Grand Central Terminal while listening to Radiohead. The other day James Taylor accompanied me on my morning bus ride. Hey, it's good to know that I've got a friend.

I've upgraded to a bigger iPod and now I've got my entire music collection on there. Rock, jazz, classical—there's something for any mood. And that's the beauty of the iPod—it allows you to select a soundtrack for the movie that's your life. It used to stress me out moving with a herd on buses, subways, and crowded city streets. But it's kind of fun now that I'm in my own private "sound bubble." Music has a way of transporting you to different times and places, and my iPod allows me to be in Times Square, present day, and Europe '72 with the Grateful Dead simultaneously. Groovy, man.

I find myself walking more since I got my iPod, and in the last six months I've dropped 30 pounds and saved a couple of bucks on subway fare. I've started writing and recording music again for the first time in years, my creative juices stirred and flowing again. Thanks, iPod!

Of course, the isolating effect of the iPod is also its greatest drawback. People already have a hard enough time connecting with one another in modern society; we don't need another gadget that further detaches us. And, yes, you shouldn't wear one while driving, or in class, and you shouldn't play it too loud, blah, blah, blah. Anything can be abused. But if you've ever sat next to a crying baby at an airport, or next to a loud-mouthed cell phone user on a bus, then you already know that a digital music player can transform an otherwise unpleasant or mundane experience into something quite magical.

The *"isolating effect of the iPod"* increased tenfold with the spread of smartphones. We cocoon ourselves in personal media bubbles. Sometimes we merge bubbles with others, sometimes we're all alone. We're becoming a hive-like society of disconnected beings. Author E.M. Forster predicted this over one hundred years ago in his short story, *"The Machine Stops."*

MODERN LIFE REFLECTS ART IN SCIENCE FICTION CLASSIC

April 2011

One of my favorite college courses was "Science Fiction as Literature" taught by esteemed professor, H. Bruce Franklin. One of the more memorable stories Franklin had us read was an obscure E.M. Forster novella called "The Machine Stops".

Forster was better known for his novels about class and cultural clashes, like *A Passage To India* and *Howard's End*. But he published "The Machine Stops" in 1909 as a response to H.G. Wells's optimistic science fiction stories. Forster wasn't so optimistic; he had concerns about mankind's increasing reliance on technology.

"The Machine Stops" is the story of a mother and her son living in a future society. People live in hive-like underground dwellings, personal "cells," and stay connected

175

through a network of computers. People rarely have face-to-face contact, and never walk on the planet's surface.

The son tries to go "off grid" and unplug from the network. He longs to walk on the surface, feel the sunshine. But robot guards, with long, metallic tentacles like Dr. Octopus, stop him.

Great science fiction has the ability to predict the future, and there's an eerie accuracy to Forster's 100-year-old tale. Not only did he predict television, the Internet, email, and instant messaging decades before they were invented, he also forecast the sense of personal isolation that accompanies these modern conveniences.

Look around. Everybody's wearing earbuds, tapping away on smartphones. People look like they're talking to themselves, until you see a Bluetooth earpiece tucked behind their ear. (Bluetooth headsets themselves are a case of life reflecting art. Those things always remind me of the headpiece worn by Billy Dee Williams' bald assistant in *The Empire Strikes Back*.)

We've never been more connected as a society. We "friend," we "share," we "like," we "post," and the web is a living history of humanity, a snapshot of current events. The Internet, and its various wireless tributaries, give shape and form to a collective human consciousness.

But, on another level, we've never been more separated from one other, each of us in a self-made cyber bubble, side-by-side but not interacting, so much like the personal cells "The Machine Stops" imagined over a hundred years ago.

Two things in E.M. Forster's story lead to society's collapse. First, as the title implies, the machine stops. Its Mending Apparatus goes haywire, leaving the computer network unable to repair itself. Second, people begin to worship The Machine in a new kind of techno-religion.

176

I'm not sure the Internet has achieved religious status yet, but it certainly fills some of the basic criteria. People believe in it, look to it for answers, and take comfort from it. It's an invisible Higher Power that seems to know and see all.

While "The Machine Stops" isn't E.M. Forster's most popular story, it echoes themes found in his other work. The motto of *Howard's End* is "only connect," stressing the importance of human interaction and building bonds with one another. If we can "only connect," Forster writes, "human love will be seen at its height." People and communities, the whole of civilization, would "live in fragments no longer."

"Only connect." It could be the advertising slogan of a wireless carrier, or a singles chatroom. But it's more sage wisdom from E.M. Forster, gaining new relevance a century later.

Keep an eye out for the Doc Ock arms.

Forster's science fiction story gets more "real" every day. But "only connect" is bad advice for modern jackasses. We don't need buttheads gathering in large groups. You know what it leads to.

Rob Errera

THE DOWNSIDE OF FLASH MOBS
AND HIGH-TECH RIOTS

November 2010

Modern technology is a wonderful thing. It allows you to stay connected with friends and loved ones, it keeps you informed, and lets you instantly share your thoughts and ideas with the entire world.

And it allows jackasses to organize.

Consider this: if you were a jackass back in 1954 and your favorite baseball team, the Giants, just won the World Series, you had to celebrate the old-fashioned way—running outside, banging pots and pans, waking the neighbors, and causing a ruckus. If you were lucky, a couple of other neighborhood jackasses might join in, helping knock over garbage cans and burn trash before the cops arrived. It was fun, but it was limited.

Today, the modern jackass has a variety of networking tools at his/her disposal to help facilitate their shenanigans. This

178

was the case last week when the San Francisco Giants won the World Series. After the winning game, hundreds of smartphone-toting fans in San Francisco logged onto Foursquare, a mobile-location service that allows you to tell friends where you are.

The message "Giants Riot on Polk St!!!" spread quickly among jackasses, as hundreds smashed windows and set fires to celebrate the team's victory. (Why? Because they're jackasses.) Even jackasses who couldn't attend the event personally were able to contribute.

"Pick up cars," a poster named Sarah W. suggested. "Set things on fire!"

Deranged fans did their best. One photo showed a man apparently trying to set fire to a city bus.

The "flash mob" is a phenomenon that has emerged with the rise of smartphones and social networking sites. A flash mob is a group of people who arrange, via various telecommunications devices, to meet at a certain place and time and do something silly, like dance "The Macarena" in Grand Central Station in the middle of rush hour. Some feel flash mobs are a type of performance art, but I hope this fad fades quickly. Unless you're chasing a monster with torches and pitchforks, mobs are generally a bad idea.

The ability to instantly organize an irrational mob is a frightening thing. Imagine if this technology were available in the 1990s following the OJ Simpson trial or back in September 2001 after the terrorist attacks. There'd be flash mobs, but they wouldn't be dancing or peacefully protesting. They'd be angry, vigilante mobs out for blood. Innocent people would get hurt.

Since 2009, Philadelphia has had at least four incidents of violent flash mobs. During these incidents, teenagers ran through the streets, vandalized property, fought with each

179

other, and attacked passers-by. Similar incidents have occurred in Boston, Kansas City, and Brooklyn. The flash mob flare-up that occurred after the Giants' win last week is more than the modern version of a rowdy victory celebration. It's a glimpse of the dark potential of social networking technology.

Add it to the list of Information Age threats, right behind Internet predators, cyber-stalkers, and Facebook bullies.

Flash mobs, bad! Clones, good!

ATTACK OF THE CLONES

January 2003

The clones are coming! The clones are coming!

Actually, if you believe the offbeat religious sect called the Raelians, the clones are already here. The French-based group supports a medical firm, Clonaid, which claims to have successfully cloned two human beings so far.

Or have they?

Clonaid representatives promised last month they would offer DNA proof, but so far both sets of parents refused to have their babies tested. And now Clonaid, which sounds like a new high-carb sports drink, is under investigation for selling false hope to parents who lost children and hoped to resurrect them via cloning. Clonaid took their money but delivered nothing.

If Clonaid seems suspicious, then its financial backers, the

Raelians, are downright bizarre. They believe cloning is the next step on the evolutionary scale, and eventually, combined with an accelerated-growth process they have yet to discover, will lead to eternal life for all mankind. The idea is you can continually grow a new host body and somehow transfer your consciousness into it. They also believe life on earth was started by extraterrestrials.

It's easy to write off the Raelians and Clonaid as wackos. They sound like most other extreme cults. But unlike the others, this group of weirdos may have actually produced a scientific miracle.

You won't be able to clone yourself anytime soon, but your grandchildren might, and their grandchildren definitely will. The sci-fi concepts of growing new organs—even new host bodies—will become a reality.

Each time a medical advance is made, a religious dogma is challenged and moral foundations are shaken. People accused the medical community of playing God when the first heart transplant was performed, and again when the first artificial heart was installed. No doubt they'll complain again when the first cloned heart is implanted, grown organically from the host's own cells. But human cloning is more complex, both morally and ethically, than any other medical advancement. The ability of man to replicate himself, "in his own image," carries a heavy responsibility.

Is cloning mankind's ultimate God-play, an attempt to mimic the power of the Creator himself? Will we be punished for our arrogance? Or is it really the next step on the evolutionary scale, mankind's ultimate victory over death, and the chance to finally become more than human?

Clonaid may not have successfully cloned a human being (or at least not been able to prove it) but someone will. That's when the rest of us will have to come to terms with the moral, ethical, and spiritual issues the Raelians have already incorporated into their belief system.

The Raelian movement is still alive, well, and waiting for our extraterrestrial overlords to return, like the Cult of Cthulu. Maybe we'll find a way off our home planet before the aliens arrive.

Rob Errera

'ROCKET SCIENTISTS' DOOM
AMERICA'S SPACE PROGRAM

August 2005

Like many Americans, I held my breath until the space
shuttle Discovery was back home, safe on the ground. It was
the first shuttle flight since the Columbia disaster in 2002,
and the nation's hopes rested on a safe return for the
similarly troubled Discovery flight.

Watching Discovery come in for a landing, I was reminded
of the final moments of the film *Apollo 13*, about a troubled
trip around the moon. The Apollo 13 crew used makeshift
tools and clever thinking in order to return home safely.

Discovery's safe return is a triumph for NASA and
America's space program. The astronauts on that flight, and
the engineers on the ground, showed courage, bravery, and
ingenuity—all the traits we look for in our heroes. When
there was a problem with Discovery's heat shield
insulation—the same problem that brought down
Columbia—the crew made tools using materials on board

the craft, made an impromptu spacewalk, and repaired the shuttle well enough to land.

But on the other hand, Discovery's latest flight highlights the massive flaws in our space program. It was a bungled, poorly planned mission. The latest shuttle repair was performed with a jerry-rigged hacksaw held together with duct tape. Duct tape! In the trunk of my car, I keep a flashlight, jumper cables, a couple of screwdrivers and wrenches, and a can of Fix-a-Flat. You need these things when you drive a 12-year-old Geo Prism. I figured the space shuttle would have an equally well-stocked tool kit on board, but that was not the case. Didn't they watch *Apollo 13*? Didn't they learn anything from the last shuttle disaster? Apparently not, since they were plagued by the same foam insulation problems. Also, Discovery was docked at the International Space Station—didn't they have any tools our guys could borrow? Please don't tell me the space station is orbiting Earth with nothing but a roll of duct tape for backup.

I'm defensive of America's space program. When my wife asks, "Why do we still send people up on the space shuttle after what happened to Columbia?" I'm quick to answer, "You can't abandon the space program!"

The exploration of space, and the idea that someday mankind may leave this planet altogether, is important. There are bound to be setbacks on our journey to the stars, but we'll never advance if we don't keep trying.

However, with the current crop of "rocket scientists" at NASA running the show, I fear our travels toward the future may be very slow indeed.

Want to speed up the space race? Take it out of the government's hands, and encourage competition in the private sector.

MONEY THE NEW MOTIVATOR IN MODERN SPACE RACE

February 2016

Money not only makes the world go around, it's shaping the boundaries of outer space, too.

A new space race is underway, but instead of global superpowers battling for military mastery of the skies, billionaire businessmen are competing to make outer space profitable.

The original space race began in the 1950s, with America and the Soviet Union battling for outer space supremacy. The Soviet Union jumped out to an early lead, putting the first satellite into orbit around the Earth (Sputnik 1, 1957) and putting the first human in outer space (Yuri Gagarin, 1961).

President John F. Kennedy upped the ante by promising America would be the first country to reach the moon. Although the US accomplished this feat in 1969 ("a giant leap for mankind"), Russia's space legacy proved far more impactful. Modern low-Earth orbiting satellites run everything from wireless phone networks to national defense systems. What have we gotten from the moon except for tide tables and dusty rocks?

The main players in the modern space race are all billionaires: Elon Musk, the magnate behind PayPal and Tesla Motors, Amazon.com founder Jeff Bezos, Virgin Atlantic/Virgin Galactic's Richard Branson, and Microsoft co-founder Paul Allen.

The new space race is fueled by the desire to make space travel "affordable," which is corporate-speak for "profitable." Developing a reusable rocket would make space travel cheaper, safer, and more efficient.

Amazon.com's Bezos is currently leading the race. Bezos founded the company Blue Origin with the dream of making spaceflight affordable in order to "seed an enduring human presence in space." In November 2015, Bezos' New Shepard rocket ship became the first rocket to ever successfully launch into outer space and land safely back on Earth.

Hot on Bezos' heels is Space X founder Elon Musk, whose Falcon 9 rocket ship (Geek Alert: The craft is named after Star Wars' "Millennium Falcon") was launched and re-landed (after several failed attempts) in December 2015, only a few weeks after Bezos' success.

Musk founded SpaceX in the early 2000s with the long-term goal of creating "a true spacefaring civilization." SpaceX started out with satellite launches, then gained multibillion-dollar contracts to deliver cargo to the International Space Station.

Richard Branson's Virgin Galactic has built/purchased several spacecraft designed for both scientific and civilian use. But the company suffered a setback last year when its

SpaceShipTwo broke up during a test flight, killing the co-pilot and injuring the pilot. Paul Allen helped finance Branson's SpaceShipOne project, and now his company, Vulcan Aerospace, is building a super-sized airplane that can be used as a platform for orbital rocket launches.

Space travel was once the restricted domain of governments. Nations employed the greatest minds in the land to probe outer space solely for the pursuit of knowledge. Today those great minds are employed by the world's biggest billionaires in the pursuit of profit.

While this seems sad and shallow, it's probably for the best. Individual entrepreneurs with vision and resources are always the driving force for change. Governments and bureaucracies slow things down and mess things up. You don't need to be a rocket scientist to figure that out.

Soon space travel will be a commercial enterprise, and a trip to outer space will be as easy as setting up a new laptop computer...

BREAKING IN THE NEW LAPTOP

April 2004

I bought an Apple iBook…for an egghead like myself, it's an exciting time.

I haven't bought a new computer in ages—the last time was 1997. In computer terms, that's "ages." I've upgraded a couple of times since then, but they were used machines, bought cheaply and upgraded as needed.

It's not only my inherent cheapness that stopped me from plunking down cash on a new computer. I'm attached to my old machines. I get nostalgic about the things I've written on different machines, the various keyboards I've worked on, sometimes pounding in frustration, other times tickling with joy. I don't know if other writers have the same kind of bond with their computers; maybe I'm weird. I feel the same way about my computer as I do about some of the guitars I've owned over the years. They're tools of creation, and they must be treated with love and respect, even when you're beating the hell out them.

Unlike musical instruments, computers are not built for lasting relationships. They're built to be replaced every few years—that's the way the computer industry keeps itself going. But it comes at a price to the environment. Approximately 30 million old computers are tossed into landfills each year, where they threaten to leak toxic metals and organic pollutants into municipal water supplies. Old computer monitors and televisions are especially dangerous—each cathode ray tube contains an average of five pounds of lead, a substance known to cause brain damage in children. New flat-screen monitors aren't much safer since they're manufactured with mercury, another known neurotoxin. Only about 14 percent of old computers get recycled, according to the Environmental Protection Agency.

If there's any life left in a computer, I'll try to find it a good home where it can live out its twilight years. The only time I'll toss a computer to the curb is if it's completely broken. As a result, there are three old computers sitting in my basement, along with a couple of printers, a monitor, and a scanner. My wife is annoyed.

Even my new laptop isn't new-new. It's a base version of last year's model being sold at a discount. Still, I am its first user, so it's new to me. The entire concept of a new computer is a misnomer anyway. If you buy a top-of-the-line computer today, there'll be a better one, a "newer" one, released within a few months. This is why landfills across the globe are filled with non-biodegradable, potentially toxic computer parts.

If computer manufacturers want to come up with a truly innovative computer, they'll make one that doesn't pollute the environment when it becomes obsolete. Automakers are introducing "green cars" that are easier on the environment. It is time for computer makers to follow suit.

Computers and related "smart" objects have yet to go green. There are still tons of plastic, electronic junk, and hazardous batteries polluting the earth…miles and miles of ancient smartphones…

HAPPY BIRTHDAY IPHONE—HIGH TECH WAXES NOSTALGIC

July 2012

Happy birthday, iPhone! For a five-year-old, you're certainly busy, popular, and productive!

I've been an iPhone user for a little over a year now, and this little device has transformed me from a mere "Apple user" to a certified "fanboy."

Several years ago I wrote a column about flip phones. I felt flip phones were popular because they looked like the communicators used by the cast of the original *Star Trek*. Everybody likes to pretend they're on the Starship Enterprise!

The iPhone has brought this piece of science-fiction future into the present. Here is a communication tool that can handle all of your needs (phone, email, text, Tweets, blogs, video chat…) as well as record audio and take notes. It's a video recorder and a still camera. You can watch television shows and movies on it. You can surf the web. It's a gaming center, and a news source. It's a banking center and a stock ticker. It's a compass. It's a global positioning system. It's a digital wallet. It's a flashlight.

But one of my favorite things to do with my iPhone is listen to music. I've got a bunch of stuff from my personal library loaded into iTunes, and I've got SiriusXM and Pandora Radio apps, too. My phone is a veritable music machine!

Sometimes I'll listen through headphones or a speaker. But oftentimes I'll let the music play through the tiny iPhone speakers. It's not the greatest sound reproduction—better than you'd expect, but still thin and tinny—but it gives me a nostalgic thrill, like I'm a kid again listening to a transistor radio.

Transistor radios were invented in the mid-1950s, and became the most popular electronic communication device in history (although I'm sure the smartphone is giving it a run). Billions of transistor radios were manufactured during the 1960s and 1970s. The pocket-size radios sparked a change in listening habits, allowing people to listen to music anywhere they went.

I had a transistor radio when I was a kid. It was red, with a wrist strap, and I'd listen to Yankee games (on 77 AM) and "New York's Home of Rock 'n' Roll" (WPLJ – 95.5FM) day and night.

That tiny radio was my window into a larger world, a chance to bring something exciting and exotic into my humdrum corner of suburban New Jersey. Radio was better than television (which, at the time, only had five channels, and a few oddball shows on UHF) because it was less predicable and required more imagination. All I needed to keep my radio going was a battery and I was good to go! (Fun fact:

193

The 9-volt battery was created to power transistor radios.) The only thing I found more entertaining than listening to the radio was reading books.

Before I even reached my teenage years, the transistor radio was eclipsed by a more powerful "boom box." Record albums gave way to cassette tapes and compact discs, and the transistor radio fell out of favor, at best incorporated into audio equipment as an afterthought. ("Bonus—Includes Free AM/ FM Tuner!")

But there's a sense of coming full circle when I listen to music on my iPhone. If I'm working in the kitchen, the basement, or the garden, I'll punch up some music or a podcast. It's never hard to find something exotic and exciting to brighten up my humdrum corner of suburban New Jersey.

The window never closes, and the more things change, the more they stay the same.

Steve Jobs' iPhone revolutionized mass communications, especially the business of writing. A smartphone is an essential part of any writer's toolbox. It has become essential for everyone, everywhere…perhaps addictively so…

SMART PHONE THE LATEST GADGET IN A WRITER'S TOOLBOX

November 2009

What is that strange man doing over there, all hunched over? It looks like he's twiddling his thumbs, or…worse. What's he up to?

Don't worry, folks. It's just me writing this column on my cell phone.

Why? Mostly to prove I can. I won't lie to you, though; it's cumbersome typing with your thumbs.

Writing is a weird profession, and writers, for the most part, are pretty weird people. It's a very solitary profession. More than half of the job takes place inside your head. People see you puttering around with something or staring into space and they think you're a flake. Hey, that's a writer at work!

Watching a writer work isn't fun, like watching an artist paint or a musician write songs. All you see is the top of a head and drumming fingers; all you hear are some occasional snorts, grunts and groans (personally, I'm a big groan/sigh fan). It's not much of a spectator's sport.

But *being* a writer is very much a spectator's sport; you have to be a spectator to life, a reporter of its events, a chronicler of its ups and down. Writers are the eyes of the world. We're not just flakes who stare into space!

As far as writing instruments go, a cell phone is a pretty weird one. Growing up, my parents had a variety of "writing machines," including a state-of-the-art Smith Corona Selectric and a funky turquoise-and-white typewriter that produced a scripted font. There was an old manual typewriter around the house when I was a kid that used a two-toned red and black ribbon on a spool, but it was a relic even in the mid-'70s. The last typewriter I used was a Brother with a little memory chip and LCD display that allowed you to edit a line of text before you printed it; high-tech for 1983.

The birth of home computers separated the idea of "writing" and "printing." Writers needed to accept their words might never "see print" but could still be read in some other format. They had to adapt again to the idea that even desktop computers and home printers are becoming obsolete. I can write, edit, and "publish" to the web all without ever leaving my seat on the bus…or my seat in the bathroom.

I've found that during a 45-minute bus ride I can usually write about 25, 160-character text messages. Depending on my inspiration level and thumb fatigue I can write 500 words on my way to work and another 500 on the way home. When I get home or to the office, I cut and paste everything together into one complete, hopefully coherent, document.

It's far from a smooth process. Sometimes there are so many type corrections and so much reformatting that simply rewriting the sentence from scratch into a proper word processor would be quicker.

But writing works in stages. The first part is getting your thoughts into words. Writers used to "put their thoughts on paper," but in today's "green world" the goal is to get your thoughts into data.

The next step, and maybe the most important, is shaping your writing. This is where the craft of writing comes into play. Real writer-types will argue that all writing is rewriting, that the style and polish you give your work is the most important part. Either way, all writing starts the same way— one word at a time, one sentence at a time. It doesn't matter if you use a word processor, a smartphone, an old Smith Corona, or a pencil and paper. Eighty percent of this column was written on an LG EnV2 flip-phone.

The hardest part of writing is finding something to say. But if you've followed me this far you know that already.

I wrote the first draft of my novel, Hangman's Jam, *on my LG EnV2 phone while commuting to New York City. I'd crank out raw text on the bus, and edit it on my laptop at home. It worked surprisingly well…and that phone wasn't even "smart"!*

WAITING FOR THE GREAT AMERICAN CELL PHONE NOVEL

March 2009

Excuse me, I feel a little queasy—I've been experiencing *keitai shosetsu.*

What's *keitai shosetsu?* A new Asian flu?

Not exactly. *Keitai shosetsu* are "cell phone novels," and they're all the rage in Japan and China. Yeah, novels written on cell phones in tiny, 100-word chunks and delivered in installments to other cell phone users.

How popular are *keitai shosetsu* in Japan? In the first half of 2007, five of the country's top ten bestselling novels were written on mobile phones, selling an average of 400,000 copies apiece. That's got Japanese print publishers happy, while Japanese literary critics decry the form as tawdry and lurid.

Now, with the rise of "unlimited texting" plans and cheap, QWERTY-keyboarded handsets, cell phone novels are making their way to America. There are already several web sites dedicated to helping people get their cell phone novels out to the public.

Will the cell phone novel fly in America? Will people take the time to bring their own inner novel to life—in tiny 140 character chunks? Seems silly, but the cell phone novel is an interesting idea for a number of reasons:

a) Writing a novel on a cell phone solves the age-old writer's dilemma of "never having time to write." You can write anytime you have a few moments and a free thumb. And it solves the reader's dilemma of never having time to read. These are novels broken down into text messages—everybody's got time for a text message.

b) The cell phone novel offers an immediacy and connection with the reader that traditional paper and ink books lack. Readers can comment on the book as it is being written and help shape its development. It's a new kind of interactive, user-directed fiction.

c) Cell phone novels are portable, and private (nobody can see what kind of trash you're reading on your handset!) and since they're downloaded directly to your phone they save you a trip to the bookstore. Plus they are enviro-friendly: no more dead trees and stinky paper mills.

d) Cell phone novels use new technology to revive an old form. Telling stories in serial form dates back to *One Thousand and One Arabian Nights;* and Charles Dickens (*A Christmas Carol*), Sir Arthur Conan Doyle (*Sherlock Holmes*), and Stephen King (*The Green Mile*) have all published serial novels. Plus traditional Japanese *keitai shosetsu* is heavy on teen melodrama; a form that never goes out of style. If the cell phone novel has an American audience it's probably among the *Gossip Girl/Twilight* crowd.

e) Once upon a time, when kings and queens ruled the land,

the poet was the top of the literary food chain; they earned the most money and commanded the most respect. Nowadays most poets can't earn enough from writing to buy a cup of latte (unless they've sold out to write advertising copy). But the cell phone's space constraints demand an economy of words that the poet is uniquely qualified to deliver. The rise of the cell phone novel could mean the rebirth of the poet…or, at the very least, a new market for crafted verse.

f) Using cell phones as a writing tool encourages more non-writers to write, and the World of Letters always needs new blood infusions to stay alive. As a writer myself, I should think that anything that gets people using written words to express themselves is a good thing, right?

Well…yeah, but…I've got some problems with this last one. Because "texting" isn't writing. There are elements of writing—word choice, sentence structure, narrative flow—that you can only learn through reading and studying how things are written. Maybe everybody has a story to tell, but not everybody has the tools to be a writer.

You are supposed to be able to write competently by the time you graduate high school. But look at 90 percent of Internet blogs, and you'll see that is not the case. Even though there are more opportunities than ever for people to express themselves as writers, people have never been more ill-equipped to seize those opportunities.

You'd think having the chance to reach millions of readers would make people *want* to become better writers, but that doesn't appear to be the case either. Japanese cell phone novelist Katsura Okiyama won a *keitai shosetsu* contest that earned her cash and a print publishing deal. But before tapping out her prize-winning story, she admits, "I had never written a story…I had never liked reading either." She developed her style writing 100 text messages a day, using the same format and tone for her fictional story.

At the risk of sounding like a pompous elitist, cell phone novels allow a lot of non-writers the opportunity to unleash their inner Stephen King or Danielle Steele, and, while I'm all for free expression, I'd rather see somebody take time to shape their writing before sharing their masterpiece with the world. Writing is a craft, a skill, a gift—you can't just "tap it out" and send it like a…a text message!

Consider this. Cheap video cameras, powerful editing software and YouTube gives everyone the power to create their own cinematic masterpiece. But have you seen a new *Citizen Kane* come out of YouTube yet? No. You see a lot of goofballs acting goofy. Cell phone novels give everyone the chance to share their writing with the world. But if you think it's a matter of time before the next *War and Peace* arrives on your cell phone you'd better hunker down for a long wait.

YouTube has yet to produce a new Citizen Kane, *but it has produced the* Karate Kid *reboot,* Cobra Kai, *which is darn close. Cell phone novels never caught on in America—we skipped right to ereader apps. Modern social media offers enough soap opera drama for most young people. Everyone is producing their own "original content" and distributing it globally via their smart phones. Everyone. That's a good thing. Right?*

WHEN AMERICAN CULTURE BECOMES AMATEUR HOUR

March 2009

My last column dealt with the Japanese literary phenomenon of cell phone novels—novels written on cell phones and distributed directly to other cell phone users. While the cell phone novel is an interesting art form for a number of reasons, I'm concerned it will open the floodgates, allowing a ton of amateur authors to glut the market with bad writing.

This is a poor attitude. Not everybody who writes needs to be a "trained professional" such as myself (a journalism degree and two decades working as a writer/editor—thank you, thank you very much). Everybody should be encouraged to put their thoughts and feelings into words, regardless of their skill level. Writing can be a powerful and therapeutic tool for personal growth and development. That's all good.

It's the *sharing* I have a problem with. It's too easy to share stuff in this modern, techno-funky society, and people are too quick to do it. It's a symptom of a bigger problem in today's world—the abolishment of the tier system, the idea you have to earn your way through certain levels of achievement before you can be considered "good" at something.

Back in the day, a writer would write something (on a typewriter or longhand) and show it to an editor or agent. If the editor/agent thought it was good, they'd shop it around to a publisher. If the publisher liked it, they'd print it and distribute it. And if the public liked it (and bought enough to make the publisher some money), then the writer would get a chance to publish another story.

A writer had to show their work to *other people*—people who knew the business of writing—and get *their* approval before their work saw print. In editorial terms it's called "weeding through the slush pile," the stack of unsolicited manuscripts submitted by writers. Only one of every ten manuscripts will be good enough to read to completion; only one in a hundred will be something worth publishing.

But now, thanks to blogs, self-publishing houses, and cell phone novels, *anybody* can write *anything* and share it with everybody instantly. It's all become one giant slush pile, and it's every man for himself (or herself) sifting out good writing from bad.

Bad writing overwhelms us, and, as a result, we start accepting sub-par compositions as the norm. Average becomes the new good, and our standards slip to a point where…well, to a point where recycled "teen confessional" trash tapped out on a cell phone can become a bestseller (in Japan, at least). A novel that was a "decent read" 50 years ago would be hailed as a "literary achievement" by today's diminished standards.

The same goes for the music business. Once upon a time, musicians had to tour extensively and get a record label to back them in order to get their music out to people. Now you can record a professional sounding album in your living room with a laptop and distribute it directly through the Internet using the same web services that big acts like U2 and Madonna use. The playing field is level for artists everywhere.

While this freedom to easily distribute your work is liberating as an artist, it also means a lot of really bad product flooding the marketplace. Would Pablo Picasso be as passionate about his art if he knew his work would sit on the same shelf alongside every other knucklehead who ever picked up a paintbrush? Would the genius of his work even be recognized there among the mediocre masses?

This erosion of quality spreads across arts and entertainment, but doesn't stop there. Standards have dropped in manufacturing and service industries, too. Are customer service people (receptionists, repair staff, sales clerks) nicer than they used to be? Are the products you buy built better and more durable? No and no.

So, in today's amateur hour world, who is going to elevate the good stuff and toss out the bad? Social media influencers? Ultimately, the decision lies in your hands. Hopefully you'll decide you still want a skilled professional to help you wade through the slush pile of product. You'll seek out the opinion of critical journalists. You'll demand better writing and support the work of talented wordsmiths.

I'll keep my fingers crossed and hope you won't see my last two columns for what they really are—a thinly veiled plea to keep my job.

I sound like a dick, and I end up fired anyway, so screw me. Twice. Instead of clinging to old writing models maybe I should adapt. The statement I made two columns ago was wrong: texting, tweeting, and emailing is writing. The job is called Social Media Editor. People younger than me are really good at it.

ANTI-SOCIAL NETWORKING: OFF-LINE AND OUT-OF-LINE

August 2010

I was at a bar recently, watching a friend's band play, when I ran into a bunch of old friends, people I hadn't seen in nearly a decade.

There were well wishes and fond-remembrances all around. But then some of my old chums chided me for my reclusive lifestyle.

"Why aren't you on Facebook?" one friend asked. "Are you, like, morally against it?"

No…well, maybe a little. I see the benefit of social networking sites like Facebook and MySpace. It'd be nice to keep in touch with friends, share info, photos, video, etc. But I have some reservations. Here are a few:

Time Sucker—Like anything worthwhile, social networking sites are only as rewarding as the effort you put into them.

That takes time, and who has *that* to spare? If I had an extra hour a day, I'd spend it working on projects I already don't have enough time for. I wouldn't spend it sending messages to an old grade-school chum, filling him/her in on everything that's happened in my life since kindergarten. Sorry if that makes me a bad person, but time is precious. I'll catch up with old classmates at the next reunion, or the next time a friend's band comes to town.

What if you don't respond to an old chum's request to be added to your buddy list? Then you're a big jerk. Suddenly you're saddled with a social responsibility you didn't ask for, and if you're not careful you can turn an old friend into a new enemy.

False Friends—What is a friend, anyway? Social networking sites produce a new kind of friend, the "cyber-friend." A main goal of social networking seems to be amassing a sizable friend-list, and getting "added" to the friend-lists of others.

It's cool having "hundreds of friends" on your page, but if you never interact with these people beyond a few text exchanges, are they really friends? A friend is someone you spend time with, share experiences with. Good friends are often those you've shared a particularly *bad* experience with. A friend is someone who helps you, whom you support in return. It's more than simply clicking "Add A Friend."

I worry young social media users have a different definition of "friend," and may find themselves lacking the skills to form rewarding relationships with real people. I'm old school. I made friends the old fashioned way, pre-Internet, when you had to talk to people, look, listen, and form a bond. You had to *make* friends. It took effort, but it was worth it because you found people who liked you for you, not because you lengthened their buddy list. Computers make our lives easier in so many ways, but I'm not sure making friends is one of them.

The Many Faces of Rob Errera—Like most people, I'm a different person at different times. I'm an Editor-In-Chief sometimes, a columnist others. Sometimes I'm a property manager, landscaper, Ebay reseller, musician, writer. My kids see Daddy, their teachers see Mr. Errera. In the privacy of our bedroom my wife calls me The Gangster of Love (and, on occasion, The Space Cowboy).

Who gets represented on my Facebook or MySpace page? And do I really want all those various facets of my life commingling? We've all been to weddings, funerals, or some other big event that produces an awkward moment, like your poker buddies chatting with your boss, wife, or mother. A social networking page creates this powder-keg of awkwardness 24/7.

I have friends who shut down their Facebook/MySpace accounts after a few months for one or more of the reasons listed above. It's easy to join a social networking site, but difficult to un-join, from what I'm told—yet another reason I'm hesitant to enter the social networking fray.

Starting a blog is on my to-do list…but I'll need a FaceSpace page to promote it.

Good idea, Einstein. Start a blog in 2010, but stay off social media. Way to read the coming trend. I finally got on board a couple of years later, and, as expected, was immediately annoyed by almost everyone.

THE MOST ANNOYING THING ABOUT FACEBOOK—YOU!

June 2014

If you don't use Facebook—congratulations! You can skip this column. The rest of you listen up.

You're annoying. Sorry, but somebody had to tell you. There are all kinds of people on Facebook, and some misuse the powerful social media site. Don't be one of the following Facebook Fails:

The Gamer

Ping! The Gamer just invited you to play Candy Crush Saga! No? How about Lucky Slots, or Farmville, or Mafia Wars? No, thanks, I'm not that much of a gamer, online or otherwise. Facebook games work like pyramid schemes or selling Amway products; the more people you get to join in, the higher your ranking. I'm glad you earned a gold coin playing Flappy Ducks. Really, I'm very proud of you, but frankly, you may have too much free time on your hands.

The Prankster

The Prankster will post something wild like, "I just used my boobs to get out of a speeding ticket!" and the first person to comment is "it," and has to post a wild lie on their Facebook page. I got scammed by the old "I ran over my neighbor's dog and tossed the body in the woods" gag. Hilarious. Rather than keep the ball rolling, I unfriended my Prankster pal. You should do the same.

The Quiz Master

What kind of tree are you? What *Twilight* Character are you? What's your Zombie Survival Quotient? What Infectious Disease Are You? Which Sex Toy Are You? What Kind of Bathroom Guest Are You? Really? It's all about you, isn't it, Quiz Master? It's all about you.

The Drama Queen

"I've reached my limit and I've had ENOUGH!" This vague, angry post demands the follow-up comment, "Gee, what happened?" which is the Drama Queen's invitation to vent about the latest injustice they've suffered at the hands of a spouse/child/boss/etc. Sometimes they skip the mystery and post a long paragraph about their problems. Don't worry if you missed today's drama; there will be an all-new one tomorrow. Drama Queens are annoying enough in real life, and equally so in cyberspace.

Honorable Mentions Of Annoyance go to the following Facebook users:

#foodpornographer — Nobody wants to see what you're eating for breakfast, lunch, and dinner!

The Optical Illusionist—"Stare at this picture for 10 seconds, type DOLT in the comments, then see what happens!" Let's not and say we did.

Guy Who Thinks Bill Gates Sitting In A Chair Holding Up A Piece Of Paper Is A Real Promotion And Shares It—Enough said.

Political Opinion Person—You're a staunch conservative. You're a bleeding-heart liberal. We get it. We don't care.

The Facebook Drunk—Friends don't let friends drink and post selfies on social media.

Here I Am Guy—Wow, you're eating at Sonic burger. You're at the mall. You're at the ballgame. So put down your phone and *be* in that place. Live in the moment and stop monkeying with your Facebook app. You can skip the little thumbnail map, too. The chances of me jumping in the car and Google-mapping my way to you are slim to none.

The Post Hog—We don't need to live life alongside you in real time via Facebook. We don't need to see your goofy profile picture in our timeline 100 times a day. Keep your posting to a minimum; less than once per day is good.

Mr. and Mrs. Obvious—"My thoughts and prayers go out to the victims of (insert tragedy here.)" Thanks. I'm glad you could make yourself a part of this terrible tragedy in some small way.

The Big Meanie—someone who posts negative comments about others on Facebook. Think all the mean-spirited things you want about your Facebook friends; just don't put anything in writing!

Oops.

Think of how you use your smartphone or tablet. You tap, hold, pinch, spread, and zoom. It feels intuitive because it's a metaphor for life itself…

PROJECT PERSONALITY — ZEN AND THE ART OF ZOOMING

June 2013

Modern software is designed to be "intuitive," to think like we do, and, as a result, our lives reflect the computer-centric world we inhabit.

Life is like Photoshop. Projects are built in layers, like an onion. One layer is the original image, another is a photo effect, another is a color correction, another is a block of text, etc. When you're done, you need to flatten the image, squeeze all the layers together to get the snapshot you're looking for. But don't forget what you're seeing is the product of many complex layers interacting with one another.

In humans, this multi-layered project is called "a personality."

One of the best examples of software reflecting life is the art of zooming. If you've ever worked with photos or video on a

211

computer, you know about zooming in and zooming out. If you have a smartphone or tablet, zooming is as easy as snapping your fingers.

The Kids in the Hall did a comedy skit back in the '80s called, "I'm crushing your head!" The "crusher" stood several feet away from the "crushee," closed one eye, and lined the crushee up between his thumb and index finger. Then he'd shout, "I'm crushing your head!" while repeatedly pinching his fingers together — much to the annoyance of the crushee.

The joke (not a particularly funny one) is about perspective. No one actually gets his or her head crushed. But the crusher achieves an all-powerful, omnipotent perspective by limiting his view of the world to a slim slice seen between the tips of his thumb and forefinger.

I'm reminded of the "I'm crushing your head!" bit every time I expand or shrink a document or photo on my iPhone. It's the same pinch/zoom, pinch/shrink ("I'm crushing your head!") gesture.

Humans inherently understand the head-crushing concept of zooming, because it's how we live our lives. During a typical day, you zoom in, focus on a specific task, and zoom out to plan what's next. You zoom in on the next item on your to-do list, zoom out when finished, and zoom in again until the list is complete (or you pass out, whichever comes first).

If you're lucky, you'll have a chance at the end of the day to zoom *way* out, and view today relative to the days, months, and years preceding it. Try to get a sense of how today fits into the overall journey of your life. Experience Zen.

It's not easy. It's a constant balancing act, something that needs to move fluidly, like a trumpet player's arm, or a photographer's telescopic zoom lens. Stay zoomed in for too long, and you obsess over details and lose sight of the big picture. Zoom out for any length of time, and you risk becoming detached, and missing those all important details.

The old saying claims "the devil is in the details," but I think God is in there, too. Look at the brushstrokes on the Mona Lisa's chin. Hear the subtle note phrasing during Vivaldi's "The Four Seasons," or John Coltrane's "A Love Supreme." Consider the mind-boggling technology needed to operate a Mars Rover, or a particle collider. These things approach perfection, approach godliness.

Tiny details make the Big Picture worth watching. But don't get mired down in them, and lose focus of the overall project—you and the life you've created.

END

Rob Errera

ROB ERRERA IS A WRITER, editor, musician, and
literary critic. His fiction, non-fiction, and essays have earned
numerous awards. He lives in New Jersey with his wife, two
kids, and a bunch of rescued dogs and cats. He blogs at
roberrera.com, tweets **@haikubob,** and his work is available in
both print and digital editions at all major online booksellers.

Non-Fiction

Autism Dad Vol. 1—Adventures In Raising An Autistic Son
Autism Dad Vol. 2—Tween Edition: Continuing Adventures
in Autism, Adolescence, and Fatherhood.
Autism Dad Vol. 3—Life Skills & Life Lessons
Santa's Little Helper Wants To Eat Your Children
Fake News And Real Bullshit
Rock 'n' Roll And Comic Books Taught Me All I Know

Fiction

Tales of Franz Rock Terror
Hangman's Jam: A Symphony Of Terror
Songs In the Key Of Madness:
New Variations On Hangman's Jam
Sensual Nightmares: Tales From The Palomino, Vol. I
The Mud Man: Mud Chronicles, Vol. 1
Other Fiction
Eight Strange Stories

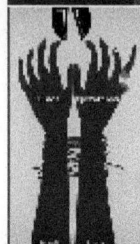

216

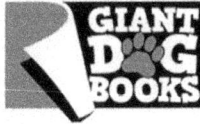

NON-FICTION   **DIGITAL BOOKS**
                     BLOGS

Autism Dad:
Adventures in raising an autistic son
Essays by Rob Errera

Autism is a complex puzzle … but Autism Dad has a clue! Funny, informative, poignant, and engaging, Autism Dad explores the initial devastation of an autism diagnosis, the autism/vaccine controversy, autism in the media, education, therapy and treatments. Above all, Autism Dad is about living with, raising, and loving a child with autism, told from a father's perspective.

"An amazing window that makes you love this family and embrace your own." — *Goodreads*

Adventures in raising an autistic son

Essays by Rob Errera

Continuing Adventures in Autism,
Adolescence & Fatherhood

Essays by Rob Errera

Autism Dad 2–'Tween Edition:
Continuing adventures in autism, adolescence & fatherhood
Essays by Rob Errera

The adventures of Autism Dad and Boy Rocco continue through the pre-pubescent years (age 8-12), leaping over autism's ever-changing obstacles, while stumbling through life's major milestones. Autism Dad and Rocco—along with Precocious Little Sister and Super Mom— tackle everything autism, from diagnosis to family dynamics, with grace and humor.

Inside Autism Dad 2 — 'Tween Edition you'll find invaluable information on:

• *The First 7 Steps To Take After Your Child's Autism Diagnosis*
• *The Basics Of Biomedical Intervention*
• *Firsthand Accounts Of The Latest Therapies And Treatments*
• *Special Needs Education And Recreation*
• *Near Death Experiences And Medical Miracles!*

Above all, Autism Dad 2—'Tween Edition is a testament to the healing power of love, and the unbreakable bond between a father and his extraordinary son.

AVAILABLE IN DIGITAL AND PRINT FROM AMAZON.COM!

WWW.GIANTDOGBOOKS.COM

www.ingramcontent.com/pod-product-compliance
Lightning Source LLC
Chambersburg PA
CBHW031954040426
42448CB00006B/356